2015
THE BEST WOMEN'S
STAGE MONOLOGUES

2015
THE BEST WOMEN'S STAGE MONOLOGUES

Edited by
Lawrence Harbison

SMITH AND KRAUS PUBLISHERS   2015

2015 The Best Women's Stage Monologues © 2015 by Smith and Kraus, Inc. CAUTION: Professionals and amateurs are hereby warned that the plays represented in this book are subject to a royalty. They are fully protected under the copyright laws of the United States of America and of all countries covered by the International Copyright Union (including the Dominion of Canada and the rest of the British Commonwealth) , The Berne Convention, the Pan-American Copyright Convention and the Universal Copyright Convention as well as all countries with which the United States has reciprocal copyright relations. All rights, including professional/amateur stage rights, motion picture, recitation, lecturing, public reading, radio broadcasting, television, video or sound recording, all other forms of mechanical or electronic reproduction, such as CD-ROM, CD-I, DVD, information storage and retrieval systems and photocopying, and the rights of translation into foreign languages, are strictly reserved.

All rights reserved.

ISBN: 1-57525-897-8
ISBN: 978-1-57525-897-3
ISSN: 2329-2709

Typesetting and layout by Olivia Monteleone
Cover Design: Borderlands Press

A Smith and Kraus book
177 Lyme Road, Hanover, NH 03755
Editorial 603.643.6431 To Order 1.877.668.8680
www.smithandkraus.com

Printed in the United States of America

TABLE OF CONTENTS

Here you will find a rich and varied selection of monologues for women from plays which were produced and/or published in the 2014-2015 theatrical season. Most are for younger performers (teens through 30s) but there are also some excellent pieces for older women as well. Some are comic (laughs), some are dramatic (generally, no laughs). Some are rather short, some are rather long. All represent the best in contemporary playwriting.

Several of the monologues are by playwrights whose work may be familiar to you, such as Don Nigro, Terrence McNally, Nicky Silver, Bruce Graham, Sharr White, Adam Rapp; Carson Kreitzer, Sheila Callaghan and Neil LaBute; others are by exciting up-and-comers such as Bess Wohl, Dominique Morisseau, Sharyn Rothstein, Dan Kitrosser, Brandon Jacobs-Jenkins, Lauren Gunderson, Nikkole Salter, Tanya Saracho, Markus Potter and Maggie Cino.

Many of the plays from which these monologues have been culled have been published and, hence, are readily available either from the publisher/licensor or from a theatrical book store such as the Drama Book Shop in New York. A few plays may not be published for a while, in which case contact the author or his agent to request a copy of the entire text of the play which contains the monologue which suits your fancy. Information on publishers/rights holders may be found in the Rights & Permissions section in the back of this anthology.

Break a leg in that audition! Knock 'em dead in class!

Lawrence Harbison
Brooklyn, NY

Dramatic
Mary, early forties

Mary Scunzio is a senior advertising executive living in a Manhattan high-rise apartment building. She is speaking to Derby, a poet who is subletting the apartment next to hers for a couple of months, and who has been in self-imposed exile in France since his wife was murdered. Mary has encountered Derby in the hallway. He appears rude and dismissive. She mistakes his insecurity and fear of contact for arrogance, and, being an aggressive personality herself, insists upon expressing her opinion. She tells him she has read his book of poetry, which moved her deeply.

MARY: Alright, alright, here's the truth . . . I bought your out-of-print marvel 'cause Google said it was a big deal when it came out and I thought it'd make me sound *cultured* to drop your name in a client meeting and then throw in a coupla lines or whatever to make it seem like you and I talk about this stuff over glasses of French wine. This is as honest as I've been in a while and it feels good, so I'm not stopping 'till I finish this little speech, even if I end up giving it to your god damned door . . . so I read the blurbs on the back and the first poem, so that I'd have somethin' to quote . . . and then I end up reading the next one, and then the next, and then the whole damn book, and then I read it again . . . I didn't know what some of those poems meant but something happened to me anyway . . . because of the sound of the words or because a phrase called up something in my memory . . . when I read "she's eggshell frail, she weighs no more than gathered autumn leaves," I saw me as a little girl raking leaves with my dad and jumping on the pile . . . but it was layered over my grandmother's last year, when she was so bent over she could hardly see me and she sobbed every time I hugged her little curved body because she had so little time left . . . and I could feel every bone of her spine through her clothes. I cry every time I read that poem. It pisses me off . . . you shouldn't be allowed to write another book if you don't give a shit that you can do that to people you don't even know.

Dramatic
Jamie, thirty-three

The boss at the sandwich shop where Jamie works has disappeared. The regional office has told the crew to stay open, that help is on the way—but help has not been forthcoming, so the crew has been buying whatever food they can and making sandwiches (co-worker Sheri's idea) in order to keep going. Finally, a guy from the head office has shown up, because someone wrote a letter which someone at his office actually read.

JAMIE: Yeah, okay, fuck, I wrote that letter. I don't know. Part of me didn't even think they even got mail in corporate. Look, I needed to cover my ass, okay? In case we got busted. Us selling people our own homemade sandwiches? I mean, that's insane. I didn't ever believe it would work. And, you know, sooner or later, I figured we'd all be out of a job. And most likely in trouble. And I, I can't really afford that right now, you know, with my kids and the court case and so I thought that if I could just, you know, seize the opportunity. Because that's what you're supposed to do, right? Stick your neck out, stand out to the guy upstairs. That's my whole point, I mean, have you ever made a Tasty Torpedo? Do you even know what's in the Southwestern Chicken? You sit there assuming, in your big corporate bubble with your assistant, like, bringing you coffee and shit—while we're here, up to our elbows in Bacon Alfredo and Artisan Breads—made by fucking machines, by the way—all for eight sixty an hour. And you guys can't even answer the phone, or show up when we need you— and then there's someone like Sheri, a person who actually has a creative idea in her head. And someone like Ted over here, who actually *cares*, who has so much passion inside him that he . . . And together, they figured out how we could still get by. Yeah, survive. Getting paid for something *we made*. That's right, these guys made—no, we all made *up*, our own sandwiches. And they are great, they are great fucking sandwiches. These people in front of you, they are the true Sandwich Artists. And I'm not just saying that, I really mean that. And then you think you can just come in here all up on your high horse, and tear down what we did? Well, I won't let you do that.

Comic
Professor Dripworth, middle-aged woman

Professor Dripworth is addressing her students on the first day of art class. She loves being the center of attention. She is flamboyant, eccentric, and nutso.

PROFESSOR DRIPWORTH:
> *(very diva and melodramatic, addressing the class)*

I feel eyes. On me. Staring. I don't like it. Look away! Everyone look away! I'm not ready!
> *(Takes a breath, composes herself.)*

Okay, I'm ready. You may view me. No, wait. It's too much. Look away! Look away!

Are you looking away? Is everyone looking away? So many eyes, all craving my artistic prowess, like turkey vultures! But how does one teach genius! How does one describe what others haven't the vision to see! Oh, the burden of being touched!
> *(shielding herself with her hand)*

Heads down! Eyes shut! Heads down, I say!
> *(Surveys.)*

There. Fine. Now we can start.
> *(Collects herself.)*

Let me begin by saying, with abject certitude, that the world will, in time, be destroyed. Of this I'm certain. By bomb, by plague, one day we will cease. So what good is painting? What good is art? When we perish, as we surely will, who will hang the Rembrandts, read the Shakespeares? I'll tell you who: *the aliens*. Look away! Heads down! DO

NOT TURN YOUR EYES ON ME WITHOUT
MY SAY!
*(Pauses. Allows for heads going down again.
Collects herself.)*

Prof Dripworth: Yes, pupils, there will be aliens. Of
this I'm certain. And, like us, they'll only preserve
art suitable to their sensibilities. So we must ask,
is our work suitable for aliens? Have we—*you*—
anything to offer our successors? This is, as artists,
our endgame: to possess talent capable of rallying
alien favor. Well, do you have such talent? This is
what you're here to find out. Right now. This in-
stant. You will draw, for the appeasement of future
colonizing life forms, what is before you. At stake:
the glory of humankind.
*(She disrobes, wearing only bra and under-
wear.)*
You may lift your heads, pupils.
(She allows them a moment.)
Look upon it, soak it in. I'm no longer your teacher,
but your muse. I'm bestowing to you the privilege
of fixing a moment in time. The way Picasso fixed
Guernica or Monet fixed the light on his lilies, mo-
ments to be captured for eons, never to be lost. So
now, pupils, make me immortal. Take up your pen-
cils, brave your souls, and etch my figure for the
alien ages ahead. Fix me!
(She strikes a pose.)

Dramatic
Emma, mid-fifties

Emma left her husband, Ulysses, 20 years ago, taking their 5 year-old son, and he hasn't seen or heard from her since. Out of the blue, she has shown up at his trailer in a trailer park in the Rockies. Here, she tells Ulysses why she had to leave him.

EMMA: When I came home from the store the house was . . . silent. Which was odd because it was dinnertime, before I left I'd put his fish sticks on the table . . . Radio'd been on, had a small roast in, all the beer was gone, but what's a roast without a little beer. You'd been sitting there with him, reading the paper, I was going to say it was perfect, but it wasn't, hadn't been perfect in a long time, but it was a . . . welcome break in the action. You'd been drinking; did I *know* you were drunk? Did I knowingly leave him alone with a, a . . . I ask myself that every day. And the house is silent and everything has been . . . swiped off the table. And I go upstairs to his room and you're . . . standing there . . . with this sort of . . . bewildered look on your face. And Sammy's in bed. Except that all his clothes are on. And I say *why are his clothes on* and you just stare at me and I think well maybe he suddenly got sick, and I, I, I say . . . *Sammy?* And he doesn't answer. And I go to him and pull the covers back and his . . . face . . . is . . . *broken.* Like . . . jagged! His . . . cheek! His ear! Just . . . broken! I'm afraid to pick him up! Like he's . . . going to fall *apart*! For years I had dreams that he's falling apart! And you're saying *it's OK*, but in this . . . REALLY . . . drunk way that sounds like . . . *ishokee. Ishokee,* and it's like this voice comes to me: run. And . . . bam! I'm downstairs. Trying to call 911, trying to keep him from falling apart, you're coming down the stairs, I grab a knife from the drawer, bolt out the door, make it to the car, you're coming out like Frankenstein, I dropped the knife or I could've *stabbed* you. So yeah, I grab you by the fucking neck. Scratch the shit out of you. And you kind of topple backwards into the mud and and . . . suddenly I'm driving. I mean did you hit him? Did you drop him? Did you shake him? Did you throw something at him? Was it an accident? Can you tell me it was an accident? Just tell me! I think you should! I think you should be able to remember why I had to go and take him like that! And I think you should remember why we had to go and spend our . . . whole fucking lives without you!

Information on this playwright may be found at
www.smithandkraus.com
Click on the WRITERS tab.

Dramatic
Toni, late forties

The family patriarch has died and his grown children have shown up at the family manse to see what if anything is left of the old man's estate. Frank (who now calls himself Franz) has gone missing from the family for years, leaving his elder sister Toni to care for dear old Dad and has appeared with his girlfriend River now that there might be some money coming to him. Frank claims that his father was crazy and that's why he had to leave. Toni lays into him.

TONI: Okay, Frank. And where was this lunatic, bipolar father these last ten years I was taking care of him? Or, better yet, the ten years before that when I was taking care of both of you? You are the last person to accuse me of abandonment. When I took you in every holiday—every Christmas, every Thanksgiving—when I was here every other month—cooking your meals, doing your laundry, breaking up fights. But this isn't about me.

(beat)

If Daddy was crazy it was because you drove him there. This man wore himself down trying to save you. We all did. Do Bo and I have a childhood home to cry over? No, because when our mother died and you started acting like a menace back in Washington, getting kicked out of every school, drinking at the tender age of thirteen, our father uprooted our entire life, our entire family, for you—to bring *you* out here—This house was supposed to save you—Because it was a chance to be good, Frank!—Which you were obviously incapable of, because guess what? I don't buy this. There is nothing new about you. Don't you see? You are not different. You are the same thing you've always been—chaos—a selfish chaos! You're doing what you've always done even now—the only man we all shared is dead, we are in mourning, and after tomorrow we will be literally left with nothing—and you thought this would be the perfect time to show up out of the blue—making this all about you and your healing with your walking rape fantasy over here—And how exactly did you think this was going to end, Frank? You apologize and we all hug it out and tomorrow, after the sale, you'd get your share? Or what? How stupid do you think we are?

Information on this playwright may be found at
www.smithandkraus.com.
Click on the WRITERS tab.

Dramatic
Louise Bauer, fifty

Louise's husband, the great German abstract painter Rudolf Bauer, he not been able to paint in 13 years. Now he is dying. She pleads with Hilla von Rehay, his former lover who built the Guggenheim Museum to house his art and from whom he has been estranged, to unblock him by telling him that she loves him.

LOUISE: I am so thoroughly tired of battling you. I'm sure I'm not the first to tell you that you are. Exhausting. And yet. I ask you here because he is dying. Soon. And I can't stand for him to approach that and be so . . . undone. I thought I would get you here to plan something big for him, give him one last show. But that's not what he needs now. That's not what we have to give. He needs *you*. He needs me too, God knows he needs me. But I can't do it alone. You charge him up. I ground him. I know this. I respect this. I have never fooled myself that you weren't half of my husband's heart. And I kept it beating while you were gone, but it's never really worked since you broke it. And that was manageable when his work was on some wall in some city, but now we three are all we have. It's just us now. And we can't hover in the past. And we can't let him die thinking he's a shadow. And maybe . . . that's why I let you in here, Miss Rebay. To say that the past doesn't matter. The future doesn't either. Tonight—Tonight is all we have. So. I think. You have to tell him you love him. *Sie lieben ihn, Frau Hilla.* Tell him this.

Comic
Rose, late twenties

Rose is sick of her life taking care of her drunken father, Curtis, and her two brothers, Billy and Ray. She takes it out on the family's pet fish, Elvis.

ROSE: Fuck you. You fucking fish. You fucking fishy fuck. You fucking fish-fucking fishy fucker. I don't know why you hang out here, you fucking fishy fucker. If I were you, I'd get the hell outta this shit-hole. I'd play dead until they flushed me down the toilet, and then I'd slosh my way through the sewage until I came out into the harbor. Then I'd swim out past the tugboats and the barges and the ferries. I'd swim 'till I got to the beaches on the big island. I'd look at all them rich folk comin' outta their big, Frank Lloyd Wright/Philip Johnson houses, wearing their blue turtle-necks and white pants, smoking big pipes, puffing pricey puffs of puffy white smoke, and drinking gin and tonics. I'd watch them get in their big, 30-foot sailboats and sail them around the bay. And then I'd move on. I'd move on until I felt the first warm currents from Mexico. And I'd follow them south. Down south to the Gulf of Mexico. I wouldn't stop until all around me was clear blue Caribbean water. Warm water. Water that feels like the sun on your back. I'd watch the tropical fish swim around. I'd see the pearl-divers diving for pearls. I'd watch ships and planes disappear in the Bermuda Triangle. I'd swim around the wreck of a 16th century Spanish Galleon, gold coins spilling out of its guts. I'd swim through the underwater ruins of ancient Aztec temples. I'd look at the ghost of Ernest Hemingway landing a striped marlin. I'd watch Panamanian drug smugglers racing by on speed boats. I'd swim through coral reefs. I'd swim around Cuba. I'd never stop swimming. *(Beat.)* I certainly wouldn't fucking hang around here. You fucking fishy fuck fish-fucking fishy fucker.

Violet, early twenties

Violet has been working as a prostitute for the local crime boss, Big Bossman, since she was sixteen. Desperately trying to escape to a better life, she asks help from Rose and her brothers, Billy and Ray. She shows them the various marks Big Bossman left on her body, some with ink, some more permanent.

VIOLET: I'm not helpless, y'know. I'm a pretty independent person. I just happen to be a little down on my luck right now, and I could use a helping hand. (Beat.) This is what he said he'd do to me. Cut me up. Like this. Into pieces. Into sections. Like you'd do with a cow. Or a chicken. This is what he said he'd do to me if I left. I don't know what kind of ink he used. I can't seem to scrub it off. I think it was a Sharpie.

(Beat. She points to a mark on her buttock.)
Can't scrub this off, either. This is permanent. He gave this to me. Burned it into my flesh. When I first came to work for him.

(She points to another scar on her chest.)
This one too. His brand, he calls it. He really has an actual branding iron he had specially made for the purpose. Like he's John Fucking Wayne in Red Fucking River. Branding cattle. "B.B." For Big Bossman. He says it's so everyone knows who his ladies belong to. And if anyone ever tries to pimp one of us out behind his back, they can't claim they didn't know what they was doing. *(Beat)* He's such a smooth operator. I'd already been a whore

in Dubai. I was just sixteen. He bought me. He acted all helpful. Bought me breakfast. Acted so concerned. Comes off so worldly, and so concerned at the same time. Like Sebastian Fucking Cabot. Said we could do business together. Said he wouldn't be like the others. Me, just sixteen. I figured working for him couldn't be worse than working in Dubai. *(Beat)* I'm one of the oldest girls working for him, now. Most don't make it as long as me. We lose our looks. Or we die. *(Beat)*Look, I'm sorry to impose on you good people. I really am. It's not my way to impose upon anybody, for anything. This is not something I do on a regular basis or anything. It's not something I enjoy doing. It's not something I'm enjoying now, delightful people though you are. I mean, I know this must be a terrible inconvenience to you all. Here you are at home, just trying to get on with your life, and in walks trouble. Someone who could get you in trouble. Who could get you in trouble with your boss. With THE Boss. I know, it's not a nice position to be put in. And I'm sorry to put you in it. Really, I am. And I wouldn't blame you at all if you were to ask me to leave. I wouldn't resent it a bit. I'd understand completely. I mean, you're under no obligation to help me. No obligation at all. That's the bottom line. You do not have to help me out. *(Beat)* But I'm asking you to.

Dramatic
Suki, twenty-three

Suki was raised in The Rev. Sung Myung Moon's Unification Church. Here, she tells her cousin about when she was "Eternally Blessed" to someone by Rev. Moon.

SUKI: My parents told me there was going to be a spring graduation ball at the East Garden. My mother took me to Saks, and bought me this little white dress—strapless, with these crystal beads. I loved that dress. She drove me to the Estate, with my best friend Mary—who also grew up in the Church. The garden was filled with bouquets of white peonies, and lit up with strings of lights. It looked magical. There were hundreds of other kids there, all our age. This really awesome band played, against the backdrop of the river, and we all danced and danced 'til sunset. Then the sun disappeared into the Hudson, and the band stopped, and Reverend Moon got up to the stage. And he announced that by the time we leave tonight, we would be Eternally Blessed to someone. At first I thought about sneaking out of the ballroom, but they had taken my cellphone at the door, and the estate is guarded by heavy security. And I didn't have any money. So, I'm trapped there. Then, Reverend Moon starts separating the crowd into men and women, as if he was parting the Red Sea. And then, he begins pointing. He points to a boy, then he points to a girl. They are matched. I'm standing there, frozen, until I see him point to Mary, who's right in front of me. She goes off with this greasy Chinese boy with acne. Then I realize it's my turn. I was shaking so hard, I could barely stand up when Moon pointed to me. By the time I look over at the men's side, three men are standing up. I had no idea which one had been assigned to me. But then, I realize he's pointing to the stage—to the lead singer guy from the band. Zeke. And he steps forward. It was a special match. And in that moment, I felt this burst of relief. It was then that I promise God I would never stray from the Church again. That I would atone for all my sins by marrying this man, this musician, chosen for me by the Messiah.

(re: her tears)

Sorry, I'm just feeling weirdly emotional right now.

Information on this playwright may be found at
www.smithandkraus.com.
Click on the WRITERS tab.

BLOOD MOON

Lila Feinberg

Dramatic
Cleo, twenty-two

Cleo is talking to her cousin, Suzi, a member of Sun Myung Moon's Unification Church, whose husband was chosen for her by Rev. Moon, challenging her belief in Moon, who members of his church considered to be the Messiah.

CLEO: You know what I'm like having a really hard time wrapping my brain around? You know what I'm trying to just like process but it's not really cohering for me? See, if the foundation of your religion is strict sexual purity, right? You know, poor Eve had dirty snake sex with Satan in the garden and now, because of that fig-leafed slut's failed one-night stand, all women are Fallen and can only be Restored by their husbands or whatever—then doesn't it strike you as, I don't know, *odd* that the Messiah Reverend Moon was arrested for conducting ritual sex ceremonies with women *other* than his own six wives? I mean, not to say that ritual sex doesn't sound like something I might want to try one day when I'm at like Burning Man or on an Ayahuasca tea cleanse, but it's got to suck for all those little illegitimate Moonie kids he—whoops!— *fathered* that they will never inherit any of his billion dollar empire. You know? But, I guess at least those women have new "spiritual bodies!" At least their wombs are cleansed! . . . That doesn't seem just a tad like . . . paradoxical to you? No? Wouldn't that just make you doubt like

---

everything you believed in if the very person who created those beliefs personally invalidated them?

Information on this playwright may be found at
www.smithandkraus.com.
Click on the WRITERS tab.

Dramatic
Jane, twenty

Jane's father, an entomologist, spends years away from home working in a rain forest. Here, he has come home for a while, and she tells him what she thinks of his being an absentee father.

JANE: Are you getting a divorce? 'Cause if you're getting a divorce, you haven't changed a bit. Do you still spend your nights dozing over a textbook in that leather chair as if you're really there? At least when you are gone, you are gone. Now you're supposed to be here, but you're gone at the same time, sort of like . . . I know! I know! You're Virtual Dad! Plug him in and pretend he loves you! Am I bothering you? Making you want to leave again? Go on. You're good at it. It will be just like all the other times you've left, only this time, you're already packed. I can hardly look at you standing by your bags. I can't tell if you're coming or going. Do you know the difference, or is there only one way for you? It's away, right? This is the moment when you swing by to tell me you're leaving again, on a longer trip with a bigger grant to study something even stranger than before, before I'm even used to having you around? I'm sorry. I guess I'm feeling cold and unwelcoming. Are you lonely for your long lost family, the one you never really wanted, or do people want families before they're formed and then freak out that they can't manage them once they get them? I don't know.

I'm just a kid. How would I know? All I know is that my adults, the ones assigned to me, they don't seem to want me around, or I can put it differently, they don't want to be around me. Ah, you say that isn't true. You say you love me, but doesn't love mean being available to a person? Most of my life I haven't even been able to call you, and forget visiting. A person needs shots and a state department visa just to get to you. But you have a great excuse, because the rainforest isn't wired for cell service. I have this thing about not seeing people in the flesh. My therapist, are you in therapy? You really should be in therapy, you know. So Mary Beth, my therapist, says I flunked Peek-A-Boo. It's that stage in development when a kid starts to trust her primary caretaker, to believe that he or she is there even if she can't see him. I flunked that part, and if a person isn't right before my eyes, I don't necessarily believe they exist. So if you really are here, and you're really not just stopping in to say you're leaving again, you're going to have to do better than this. Silence, your silence, isn't working for me.

Information on this playwright may be found at
www.smithandkraus.com.
Click on the WRITERS tab.

Dramatic
Emily Mancini, thirty

Emily is a wry, self-aware woman coming to terms with a crumbling marriage and the fact that life at 30 doesn't look like what she thought it would. She has returned home in the aftermath of Hurricane Sandy to help her parents salvage what they can from their destroyed house. Here, Emily is sharing coffee cake with her mother and her mother's best friend Mary, who has just asked Emily how she's doing in the wake of her recent divorce.

EMILY: Actually, I'm enjoying being alone for a while. I *am*. It's peaceful. Clean. You never get home to find somebody left the dishes in the sink or finished watching *Game of Thrones* without you then *deleted* them all or ate the whole tub of hummus then put the empty container back in the fridge as if they didn't *notice* they'd finished it. They ate a whole thing of hummus without once even looking down into the container and seeing that it was empty? And then they just put it back so that you'd think there was still some left if you were counting on that for oh I don't know, maybe a little much-needed, much-deserved post-work snack? Not to mention, who even eats a whole tub of hummus? That's a ridiculous amount of hummus. But now? If I purchase a tub of hummus, there's my hummus! Sitting there when I open the fridge, exactly as I left it. Completely full and waiting for me to enjoy. And I can have as much as I want because there is no else there. I am alone. I am utterly and completely alone. Except for my hummus. Just me and my hummus.

Information on this playwright may be found at
www.smithandkraus.com.
Click on the WRITERS tab.

Dramatic
Luisa Maquin, late twenties to thirties

Luisa, a Guatemalan coffee farmer, is broken but still resilient. Abandoned by her husband after their new born daughter suddenly dies, she speaks out the window to him after he may have mysteriously left flowers at her sill. She lifts the window open and yells.)

LUISA: *MMMMMAL PARRR-IDDDOO! Sin verguenza! Desgraciado!* Won't call you by your name. Don't deserve my lips to speak it. You can't float in two places at once. Can't be dead and living all at the same time. Pick one. Dead, *bueno*, be dead and never come back. Leave me with our child. The living one and the dead one. You carry the dead one. You willed it as you said. Prayed that it would end before it began. As you drank -vomited, drank-vomited, drank-vomited, over the bathroom hole I lay there in our bed breathing hope into our little girl. Quickly I brought her to my breast, wrapped my arms round her and then . . . her head fell into my hand. Was it you, that only let her stay with me one night?! Your fear of being trapped by this land. Another mouth-walking on this land. Hungry. *(beat)* Or was it me? Is it? Is it? *Que es?!* You could have just let me go on thinking that it was me. That she left me, that my arms were not enough. Do you watch us? From corners still, you watch . . . leaving your tracks after you've left. A wild dog leaking it's toxins still. Or do you want to live? Be living here with me and Pablito. That's good enough, to slither in at night, to be a hungry ghost to your own son? A hungry husband. Lingering around my hungry heart. Lay these flowers at the grave of our daughter. Angelica, yes I named her. I gave IT a name, the thing you dreaded the most, I named. So you can never disappear her from me. That which is named, lived. The whole night she breathed on me, the perfect child, her little eyes opened like roasted beans. Her tiny hands reached for my face, she entered this world with a crying chaos, and even as breath left her, she knew she was safe. At home. I cradled her a grave peacefully out of this world. But your drunken bathroom hole confessions, your whispering to me in your stench of breath, ended her breath. You willed it. If your will could kill our daughter? If you love us you will make it grow back. You will make Pablito's finger come back to life. He will wake up with his whole finger, do you hear me?! Do—do you—Do you hear—me . . . mmmeeee . . . .

Information on this playwright may be found at
www.smithandkraus.com.
Click on the WRITERS tab.

Dramatic
Wang Min, thirties, Chinese

Wang Min, a Chinese conceptual artist, is speaking to an interviewer onstage, in front of an audience. The interview follows the performance component of her theater/art hybrid installation piece that takes the audience through several levels of deception. Here, she describes her initial influence for the piece.

WANG MIN: The piece was first inspired by the many incidents of scandal involving lying and plagiarism in the United States. Recently Jonah Lehrer, then James Frey, Stephen Glass. But I was particularly interested in the Mike Daisey scandal that occurred here about a year ago. Okay, so he goes on this program to talk about the Chinese workers, and receives a lot of publicity for this, and then when the host, this Ira Glass, is told of the inaccuracies, Daisey is brought in a second time and is in essence . . . crucified on the air for lying, by Ira Glass and the reporter who uncovered him. One of my main points of interest has always been America's relationship to truth, particularly in relation to other countries. America places a high premium on "truth." No persons of any other culture get more defensive when questioned over their "truth." This piece of journalism must be absolutely, empirically *true*. This piece of art must be emotionally *truthful*. So when a glitch in "truth" occurs, the impulse is to defend and argue your own "rules of truth" to the death. And in the meanwhile the real *content* of truth-workers' conditions in China-gets sidelined in the conversation. This is what captured my imagination-how arcane American truth battles reveal the hollowness of her global outreach. So Mike Daisey is a theater artist; and as per his perceived rules of his medium, he allows himself to stretch truth in order to craft a compelling narrative. But when placed in the context of *NPR* and *This American Life*, he runs into problems. Different medium, different rules. There has been a lot of this. Take James Frey for example, who is crucified by Oprah for his book *A Million Little Pieces*. Again, a confusion of category—if he had called it a *fictional* memoir, no problem. Nonfiction? Big problem. What interests me is this rift that occurs when different sets of rules bump against each other. We open a great chasm of unknowing. We see we do not know anything other than the architecture of our own rules. So it is this rift I seek by mixing theater with visual art.

Information on this playwright may be found at
www.smithandkraus.com.
Click on the WRITERS tab.

Dramatic
Wang Min, thirties, Chinese

Wang Min, a Chinese conceptual, is speaking to an inter-
viewer onstage, in front of an audience. The interview fol-
lows the performance component of her theater/art hybrid
installation piece that takes the audience through several
levels of deception. Here, the theatrical world around her-
self and the interviewer has grown surreal, and she has
become a spiritual guide of sorts.

WANG MIN: A lie is not a bad thing. It is a natural oc-
currence and is totally understandable. Jayson Blair,
James Frey. Why did they lie? Because a lie is a new
home. A place of return after long and lonely jour-
neys in the dark. Now comes the point in the work
where we recognize the interview has changed into
something else. Something new. We're unmoored
now. Adrift at sea. We are witnessing the birth of a
new lie as we speak. We see how in our search for
truth we move into something artificial once again.
How do we escape lies? A lie is a garden that grows
sideways until its sideways-ness becomes straight.
It is a feast made from mislabeled ingredients that
tastes incredible. It is a documentary. A dollar bill.
It is thinking outside the box but then being inside the outside of the box so going further going
outside the inside of the outside of the box by going back inside the box to be outside the outside of
the box then leaving the box to find another box
whose outside has an outer outside outside, outside
the outside. It is not a matter of end goals, meaning,

landings. It is only a matter of journey. And that is the point. We negate and keep negating. To stop this thread from unwinding is to rest inside a lie.

Information on this playwright may be found at
www.smithandkraus.com.
Click on the WRITERS tab.

Dramatic
Maggie, thirty-three

Maggie lives near Chalk Farm in West London, the scene of a recent riot. She's worried that her son, Jamie, may have participated in it. She works in the claims department at an insurance company, presently dealing with claims as a result of the riot. She tells of a particularly angry claimant.

MAGGIE: I get this call through from this woman who's, like half screaming, half-crying. You get that sometimes when they've been sitting in a queue for long enough, you learn to live with it. But it's near the end of my shift, I'm cream-crackered and the woman she comes through all tight, squeaky voice and shuddery breath and I ask her address and she says 72 Adelaide Road. And I'm asking her what she's claiming for and her voice goes even higher and she's saying she knows who's smashed her windows. She's saying, it's those wasters and pigs over at the Chalcot's estate. Chalcots. Where my Jamie is sleeping in the little flat what I work and work for to live in a respectable area like what Chalk Farm is. And my mind is watching over my Jamie's room, the piles of clothes, the mess on the floor, the window we used to look out of. And then her voice starts to shake and rattle like her head's about to blow off and she's off on one going "scum of the earth, pigs, no right to live here amongst good law abiding citizens, should be hounded up and locked away or worse" and she's screaming now, proper yelling. And all I can see is my little Jamie in dim light with the curtains closed breathing softly like an angel and I'm thinking: you don't know. You don't know him. You don't know who he is. I see him, I'm his bloody mum alright. And I'm thinking how she's probably passed me in the street, she's probably passed Jamie in the street, and I'm imagining the things she's thinking as she walks past. Swine. Scum of the earth. Pig. Chav. And I'm thinking: well, what if he did do your window in? What if he did and so he should, that'll fucking teach you. So it's pigs is it? It's chavs is it, up in Chalcots? Well fucking fine then, let's have your windows and the rest of you if that's how it fucking is!

Dramatic
Destiny, early twenties, Liberian

Destiny, a former child soldier in Liberia, has come to the United States as an undocumented refugee, where she struggles to navigate the battlefield of an inner-city high school while keeping her past a secret and striving for an education. She has learned that her friend, Martina, a gang member, is HIV+. She refuses to take Martina's baby, Sofia, should Martina die, because she prefers to remain focused on her education. This refusal of the child catalyzes her recollection of what happened to her own baby when she was a child soldier.

DESTINY: You were only a few months old. But already such a bright little girl! Laughing and chattering such pretty sounds. How I loved you! I would have gladly given my life for you, but it wouldn't have helped. It was time to go out fighting again. They gave us drugs, slitting our foreheads with razors so cocaine would go directly into the bloodstream. Then they performed the ritual to make us brave. There you were, the next one to be sacrificed. He picked you up. I screamed and cried, but he held his knife to my throat and said he'd kill me, too, if I made one more sound. He slit your throat, a flash of unbearable pain, while a soldier about my age held a cup to collect your blood. My own flesh was on fire. The cup was passed around for all of us to drink. I drank without thinking. My eyes were only on you, as you slowly stopped crying and wiggling and breathing, the last drops of blood dripping out your chubby little neck like water from a leaky tap.

Then you were still, so still. Your blood ringed my lips as I rushed forth to gather you in my arms, but they wouldn't even let me hold you once more. His knife was in my back as we carried our guns out into the bush. I turned back to look at your little body, a naked scrap of promise lying in the dust. He prodded me, forcing me to turn around, mixing your blood with mine. The scar is all I have left of you. How I long to hug you, kiss you. It hurts. It hurts so much.

Information on this playwright may be found at
www.smithandkraus.com.
Click on the WRITERS tab.

CHILD SOLDIER
J. Thalia Cunningham

Dramatic, Contemporary
Destiny, twenties

Destiny, a former female child soldier from Liberia, has come to the United States as an undocumented refugee, where she struggles to navigate the battlefield of an inner-city high school while keeping her past a secret and striving for an education. A former rebel general, now a pimp, promises to get her a green card in exchange for her services as a prostitute. Meanwhile, she is haunted by three spirits from her past, who rekindle her awareness of her former life.

Notes: General Machete Mouth, a former rebel commander, now in the US under suspicious circumstances and a pimp, has demanded that Destiny "be nice" to Charles, a former member of the UN Peacekeeping forces in Liberia. When Charles begins undressing Destiny and sees the initials scarred into her chest and back by Machete Mouth, he asks her about her former life.

DESTINY: Ya. My brother Matthew first. He was my best friend as well as my brother.
I helped him with his schoolwork; he fought the older children when they teased me.
The rebels attacked our village.
One of them tied a rope around my mamma, my younger brothers and sisters, and me.
It bit into our flesh.
Then the kerosene.
They held a gun to Matthew's head and told him to light the match.
His eyes met mine, looking at me as a big brother should look at his little sister.

Gentle. Protective.

His hand shook as he tried to light the match.

Then, suddenly, he threw the flame at the rebel who held the gun, while lunging at the knot in the ropes to free us.

It was over in seconds.

I felt the shot, rather than hearing it.

The back of Matthew's dear head exploded, and my lap became warm and sticky, as his blood and brain matter flew around us.

The rebels looked at the group of us, still knotted together with the rope.

I was the next oldest.

As they pried me out and re-tightened the rope, Mama squeezed my hand.

It was the last time I ever felt her touch or heard her sweet voice.

She whispered one last thing to me.

Then the rebels gave me the same chance they gave Matthew.

What could I do?

I was warned not to cry.

(crying)

Oh, mama! I'll hear all your screams in the flames for the rest of my life.

(she stifles her crying)

Please! Don't tell General Machete Mouth. I'm sorry, I'm sorry.

Mama told me, "You're my strong, smart girl. Make us proud." Such love in her voice.

(crying again)

Papa was out in the bush.

I prayed they'd take me and leave, but they waited for his return.

How stupid I was when they asked, "Is this your

father?"
Then they handed me a machete.
Like butchering a goat.
Papa! Please forgive me!

Dramatic
Destiny, early twenties, Liberian

Destiny, a former child soldier in Liberia, has come to the United States as an undocumented refugee, where she struggles to navigate the battlefield of an inner-city high school while keeping her past a secret and striving for an education. General Machete Mouth, a former rebel commander, now in the US under suspicious circumstances and a pimp, has demanded that Destiny "be nice" to Charles, a former member of the UN Peacekeeping Forces in Liberia. When Charles begins undressing Destiny, he sees the initials scarred into her chest and back by Machete Mouth and asks her about her former life.

DESTINY: Ya. My brother Matthew first. He was my best friend as well as my brother. I helped him with his schoolwork; he fought the older children when they teased me. The rebels attacked our village. One of them tied a rope around my mamma, my younger brothers and sisters, and me. It bit into our flesh. Then the kerosene. They held a gun to Matthew's head and told him to light the match. His eyes met mine, looking at me as a big brother should look at his little sister. Gentle. Protective. His hand shook as he tried to light the match. Then, suddenly, he threw the flame at the rebel who held the gun, while lunging at the knot in the ropes to free us. It was over in seconds. I felt the shot, rather than hearing it. The back of Matthew's dear head exploded, and my lap became warm and sticky, as his blood and brain matter flew around us. The rebels looked at the group of us, still knotted together with the rope. I was the next oldest. As they pried me out and re-tightened the rope, Mama squeezed my hand. It was the last time I ever felt her touch or heard her sweet voice. She whispered one last thing to me. Then the rebels gave me the same chance they gave Matthew. What could I do? I was warned not to cry. (crying) Oh, mama! I'll hear all your screams in the flames for the rest of my life.

(She stifles her crying.)

Please! Don't tell General Machete Mouth. I'm sorry, I'm sorry. Mama told me, "You're my strong, smart girl. Make us proud." Such love in her voice. *(crying again)* Papa was out in the bush. I prayed they'd take me and leave, but they waited for his return. How stupid I was when they asked, "Is this your father?" Then they handed me a machete. Like butchering a goat. Papa! Please forgive me!

Information on this playwright may be found at
www.smithandkraus.com.
Click on the WRITERS tab.

Lawrence Harbison   51

Dramatic

Jenny, twenties to forties

Jenny Masterson is a TV reporter who lives both in reality and in Dave Tamzah's paranoid fantasy world. He has recently blown up his workplace and accidentally killed four co-workers, but no one knows it yet. In this scene, Jenny has just crawled out of the television set in Dave's living room. Dave demands that she go back. During this monologue, she and Dave are engaged in an all-out brawl as she attempts to drag him back into the television. She is beautiful, terrifying and brutal.

JENNY: You don't really mean that. See, I possess a down-to-earth friendliness that encourages people to welcome me into their living rooms, kitchens, and bedrooms. The women see me as a slightly better-looking, thinner version of their friends. And the men, well, I appear chaste, but not so much that you can't imagine us . . . It's time for you to show me a proper welcome, Dave. I'm lively. Didn't you see me cooking fried clams at the diner? Or sliding down the pole at the fire house? Running the 10K for breast cancer? Dog grooming? I'm fun, fun, fun. You think it's easy to tell people bad news all the time? Evil and danger are lined up around the block. We just give you the teeniest, tiniest, itsy bitsy, little taste of the crushing wall of pain that's about to fall on you. You want a harmless little flirtation, maybe even a brush of lips to lips, our breath intermingling, a hand in my hair. But it's not harmless, is it? Harm has been done. You don't understand—once I'm here, I want to go for a ride. And once I'm on board, we are going for that ride until I'm satisfied. And I'm not satisfied until you beg for mercy. Feisty. I like that. But also unrealistic, disrespectful and elitist. Too good for me? You don't get to make the rules, see? Once you're in the game, you play by my rules. Got it? We're all in the game. And especially someone like you. Sweety. Lover. You like it rough, don't you? Oh, no, come back here. I don't let go easily. On TV, they look like fingers, but they're claws. Ask anyone. There are plenty out there with scars to prove it. Which is it? You want me, you listen to me, you disown me? Which is it? Which is it? Do you love me? That's what they say. I love my wife. The other stuff was just—what? Physical? Meta-physical? Media? The rest was just the news-cycle, honey. Cast me off like a ten-dollar crack whore. But when the storm blows in, and it is com-ing, don't kid yourself, lover boy, when it comes you're going to try to have it both ways—you're going to ignore me and blame me. "It wasn't me. It wasn't my fault. It was Jenny. Big, scary, Jenny. Jenny with her non-stop gloom and doom, her lit-any of murder, rape, degradation, danger, danger, danger."

(Belches a huge belch.)

Sorry. Remnants of the last poor sap I ate for break-fast.

Dramatic
Abigail, sixteen

Abigail's mother is a tour guide at a natural history museum. Formerly a confirmed atheist, Abigail has begun to question the facts about evolution which she spouts during her tour. She has started to wonder if, behind evolution there is intelligent design. Abigail is autistic. Mrs. Cohen is the head of the museum.

ABIGAIL: I want to explain Intelligent Design—but I'm not very good at explaining things, so I'm going to explain it like I'm Mother giving a tour. That's called pretending. Mrs. Cohen said pretending is good for kids, even if it's hard for them to do. I'm going to pretend now. Hello, my name is Abigail. Now let's start at the beginning, a very good place to start. Who knows what that's from? "The Sound of Music." Oh, everyone here is so smart. In the beginning, there was this big bang. And then the earth was made and then man and here we are. But the reason there was a big bang at all is because there was a designer, a designer who made everything happen. And I'm not saying that this designer is God or anything, because if I say it's God then people say it's not science and they get all angry. So it's just a designer. But this designer made time and space and he made evolution, too. But there are things we don't know about evolution, things even our smartest scientists can't figure out. And that's where the designer comes in. Like eyes. Eyes are really, really, really complicated. In order for eyes to work, certain parts would have to be made before other parts in the exact right order or we'd all be blind. Now how could evolution have come up with something like that? How could our eyes have come from just the single cell—without help from . . .

(She stops.)

Okay, I have to stop pretending now. My favorite book is "Darwin and the Turtles." It's for kids, but only really smart kids can understand it. I've read it a hundred and six times. If you read "Darwin and the Turtles," you would understand that what I've been saying is stupid. Because everything could come from one cell. It would just need to take a really, really long time. And fifteen billion years is a really, really, really long time. And some people aren't made like everyone else. Some people are made different and other kids make fun of them and what kind of designer would design a person like that? What kind of designer would design a person like that? What kind of designer would design a person like that?

Dramatic
Victoria, forties to sixties

Victoria is the head of a natural history museum. She is upset that one of her tour guides, Claire, has begun to include thought about Intelligent Design in the spiel she gives on her tour.

VICTORIA: We used to have freedom in this country. We used to be able to smoke and - and not wear a seatbelt and ride a bicycle without a helmet. Orwell was wrong. The government hasn't become our big brother, it's become our mother. All right, you see this folder. These are letters, all requesting—no, demanding to meet with me. Do you know who they're from? Creationists. Wait, that's not what they call themselves nowadays—let me make sure I get this right—

(Checks a letter.)

Ah, they're Young-Earth Creationists. That's right, Young-Earth Creationists. Sounds like an unfortunate folk group from the sixties. And they believe that the Bible is a document of fact and the earth is exactly 6,000 years old. They think all of our scientific knowledge is just, I don't know, silly. So what do these Young Earthers want from me? They want our tours to include their creationist myths. But I won't even meet with them. You picked the wrong time to do this to me, Claire. There's this new member of the museum board. A man named Kringle. That's right, Kringle. Never trust a man with the same last name as Santa Claus. He's some rich entrepreneur who bought his way onto the board. Fine, he wouldn't be the first asshole with an agenda to buy his way onto the board of a cultural institution. Well, a couple of months ago, after sitting there quietly for nearly a year, Mr. Kringle asked why doesn't the museum deal with the scientific debate on evolution. Notice the sneaky adjective he used—scientific! And I said we don't deal with it, because it doesn't exist. There is no scientific debate on evolution. Not one legitimate scientist on the planet questions evolution. Not one. When you, of all people, tell me there are problems with evolution . . . There are no problems! There is no evidence against evolution—none! You hear me? None! And I will not! I will not! I will not have that thought in this museum!

Dramatic
Abigail, sixteen

Abigail's mother, a tour guide at a natural history muse-um, has been including thoughts on Intelligent Design in her spiel about evolution, which has gotten her in trouble with the head of the museum, who has ordered her to take a few days off. Abigail is autistic. This is direct address to the audience.

ABIGAIL: I'm staying with Aunt Joanne for four and a half days. I like staying with Aunt Joanne. She never comes in and checks what website I'm on. Last night, Mother and Daddy decided to go on vacation, even though they didn't have plans and Daddy's work was going to yell at him for not giving them any warning. They drove down to Myrtle Beach, and Daddy was afraid our car wouldn't make it because it's an old piece of crap. I'm not allowed to say shit but I'm allowed to say crap. When I got back from school, I went on www-Facebook-dot-com even though I'm not allowed to go on www-Facebook-dot com—His name is Danny. He lives in Indiana and takes a special class like me and his favorite show is "American Idol" and my favorite show is "American Idol" and some-times kids call him retarded even though he's not and sometimes kids call me retarded but I'm not. His name is Danny. Danny. Danny. Danny. Danny from Indiana and me IM'ed for two hours and forty six minutes until his mother told him he had to get off the fucking computer. That's what she said, not me. I told him all about me. And Daddy. And that Mother was in trouble. And he said for what? And I said do you believe in God? And he said—of course, everyone believes in God. I said not me. And he said I should because his mother takes him to church every Sunday and if he gets too loud she lets him play his Gameboy and sometimes he gets too loud just so he can play his Gameboy and of course there's a God because why else would everyone go to church. And I said did you ever read "Darwin and the Turtles" and he said he hates reading books because they give him a headache and I said you should read "Darwin and the Turtles" even if it makes your head hurt and he said okay. Okay. Okay. He's my best friend. My best friend. My best friend. I think I love him.

Dramatic
Rain, mid-twenties

Rain's fiancé Jeremy has told her a horrible story about his childhood, which involved the ancient stone marker they are standing in front of. Rain tries to comfort him as best as she can.

RAIN: If I could blast that stone into a million pieces, I would. If I could reverse the mortar and the flow of time, I would return that stone to dust. And water. From whence it came. For you to have to look at something so unmoving, so . . . cold . . . But if I did that, Jeremy, if . . . I destroyed that stone . . . What if I lost you in the process? What if I never met you? What if . . . ? When my mother died I . . . She was holding me just like this. Her arms across my chest. The tornado flattened everything. Our house, our . . . neighbors . . . She held me many hours before I realized she was gone. I couldn't talk because . . . she was holding me so tightly. I couldn't move because . . . she was holding me so tightly. For sixteen hours, I couldn't move. I . . . was pinned in this position. From the time the twister hit until . . . I thought that she was mad at me. I thought that she was . . . She wouldn't let me go. It took twenty men to get us out of there. Twenty men to lift a *house* from off of my mother's back. The refrigerator . . . Stove . . . Even after she was gone, she . . . protected me. She shielded me. She kept my body warm. Your mother loved you, Jeremy. She never left you. She couldn't stop the storm from coming, but . . . she never left your side. The daffodils were protecting you, shielding you. Keeping your body warm. I'll never let you go, Jeremy. I'll never let you go.

Comic
Veronika, late thirties, African-American

Veronika, a home care nurse, tells her latest charge, Carolyn, who's dying of cancer, about an incident that occurred when she worked in the emergency room at a hospital.

VERONIKA: Yes ma'am, I saw a lot of weird stuff in the ER, but that tops'em all. In fact, that's right about when I decided to get into caring for the elderly. Shit. Old people are generally wise enough to know a watermelon's got no place up their ass. You gotta appreciate the man's sense of adventure, though. I bet he's a real hoot in bed. Or in the produce aisle— ha! If he worked at a grocery store and got an employee discount, that'd be like an endless sale on sex toys for him. That'd be some shit, wouldn't it? You think his coworkers ever suspected him of being food fetishist? Can you imagine? "Mr. Smith, is that a cucumber in your pocket or are you just happy to see me?" HA! That wasn't his name, by the way— Mr. Smith. I changed the name to protect the . . . well I was gonna say the innocent, but I think a watermelon up the ass pretty much precludes you from that category. Hell, the watermelon may've been the only innocent party up in that camp. Still. I wouldn't put the man's business out on the street like that. It's illegal. And unprofessional. And I am nothing if not professional.

Sericomic
Veronika, late thirties, African-American

Veronika, a home care nurse, is having difficulty coping with her latest charge, who's dying of cancer. Here, she prays.

VERONIKA: Okay, God. What kind of shit is this you're trying to pull? Are you testing me to see just how much I can take before I get back in bed with the Devil? Or is this a legit mission you want me to accept? I mean it's not like you give signs like you used to . . . burning bushes and whatnot? That's unmistakable shit. But what do I have to go on? I'm *willing* to do *your will*. Know that. Even if it means budgeting for the rest of my life, turning down twenty-seven *millio* . . . you know what, I'm not even gonna say that out loud any more. It's just . . . it's cruel. If your will is that I say no to all that, it's cruel, but . . . it's *done*. Just *please*: let me know. I'll admit, "Thou shalt not kill" . . . that's pretty clear. But not too long before that mandate, you were commanding your disciples to take out their own fam, so clearly there's a gray area. Is that where I am right now? The gray area? Is the gray area supposed to feel like an episode of the Twilight Zone? Look, I know you probably get this a lot, but as this really is a matter of life or death, I don't think one little sign is too much to ask. God . . . ?

(Silence. Punctuated by a wicked loud fart. It surprises Veronika even though

it came from her. Yup. One of those.)
Really? Don't tell me that's it! How am I even supposed to interpret that? You know what? Forget it.
Forget I asked. I'm just gonna . . . I'm just gonna
spray some . . . spray some spray shit and keep
moving and all will be revealed. I have faith. I do.
Watch how faithful I am . . .

*(Over all this, Veronika has retrieved a can
of aerosol from somewhere and is spraying to
cover up the fart.)*

I'm just gonna keep on doing what I was doing
until you show me I should be doing otherwise.
I'm gonna . . . I'm gonna scrub the *fuck* out of this
tub, for starters. And I'm gonna rinse it when I'm
done scrubbing, and when I'm done rinsing, I may
just scrub it again if it'll keep me from putting
that old spider-bitch in a choke-hold and giving
her what she's been asking for . . .

Dramatic
Kathy, Forties

Kathy is a bartender by night, where she met June and Loomer, who were drinking at her bar. When Loomer faints, Kathy drives them to her house, where they can sleep the night off. But sensing that June needs saving, Kathy offers her a worldview that embraces the Light in the world as they drive in the dark night.

KATHY: I used to drink every night. Every single night. And then I'd drink every morning too. And afternoon. And whatever's that time between afternoon and night. I had a baby girl and a baby boy. And one night, drunk as a skunk, I took them for a ride on my little skiff. And I was so drunk and the air was so salty and the night was so cold and dark and I kept thinking, I am in complete control. I can do anything in this darkness. I can and sing and shout and jump up and down. And I did. I jumped up and down on that little rowboat and like a catapult, it shot my kids out in the dark, dark water and they never found them. To add insult to injury, police even claimed I killed 'em on purpose. I had to do something pretty terrible to throw 'em off the scent. It was a dark, dark night as he was badgering me and I felt as though I should just give up, you know, give in? But suddenly, suddenly there was the moon. And it shone so bright it lit up my porch like it was day. There was Light and I suddenly felt like I could choose life and so I did. And I fooled a man that could easily be fooled.

The particulars are unimportant but the point is laid low, created a new identity, changed my name from Cathy with a C to Kathy with a K and never turned back. It was all darkness, June, and I was lost. But now? Now I let Light make all the decisions for me, and I haven't lost a single thing yet.

Information on this playwright may be found at
www.smithandkraus.com.
Click on the WRITERS tab.

Comic
June, twenty

June and Loomer have just run away from a crime scene, where they were the witnesses to a double murder. June, who has a secret of her own, wants to coerce Loomer into taking on a new identity.

JUNE: We can't have people calling us, or coming after us, okay? We have to be completely untraceable. We have to create new lives for ourselves, Loomer. Everything you once knew about yourself you have to change. Your name, your age, your history. All of it. Okay, my name is going to be something nice, something wonderful. Something like Rosemary, but different. Harpsichord. Harpsichord Hall. Muth. Harpsichord Hallmuth. Okay? And you're my husband. Rick. Lo. Ben. Ton. Ricklobenton. Ricklobenton Hallmuth. Okay. And where are we from? Where are we from, Loomer? We have to be from somewhere. Maybe we're from, I don't know . . . Idaho! Yes, we've been struggling potato farmers. And we're out east because we're looking to start growing parsnips. No, no one would buy that. Turnips! And we met on a cruise, I was dancer at sea and you were on your honeymoon with an unidentified Hollywood starlet. But she only cared about her career and you wanted her to work on your farm and then you saw me in a little burlesque number while we were rounding the Caribbean Sea, and the number was called "Potato Skins" and it was very sultry.

...d you fell in love with me and I came back to Idaho and became a proper woman until a potato famine struck which threatened not only our livelihood, but our very marriage. You took to drinking and I delved into color-by-numbers water-coloring. It wasn't until we saw an ad for turnip farming that we finally faced ourselves in the mirror and said, "We have to do this. We have to go out there and change. Not just for our business. But for each other."

(She takes a breath.)

That's a beautiful story, isn't it? Just came up with it, like right on the spot. You think you can remember it?

Information on this playwright may be found at
www.smithandkraus.com.
Click on the WRITERS tab.

Seriocomic
June, twenty

After June and Loomer witness a double murder, and June refuses to call the cops, she begs Loomer to change his identity with her. When Loomer presses her as to why, June finally reveals her deep dark secret.

JUNE: We cannot go to the police! BECAUSE I KILLED JIMMY, OKAY?! I killed him! I killed him with that stupid boat vase! We were at a flower show in Buxton and there was a blue-glass vase I really liked that had a picture of a boat on it. I liked it cause who puts a picture of a boat on vase? And so that night, Jimmy came home and he had the vase and he put it on the counter and I was like, Oh Jimmy. And he was like, Oh baby! And I said, that was so thoughtful. And I was getting really excited, cause maybe this blue glass boat vase was his way of telling me he added what was needed to my savings and bought the boat. But he had that glum look in his eye, which always makes me feel bad for him, even though it means he's done something awful and then he says, Baby, there's something I have to tell you. You know all that money you saved for your little boating trip across the Atlantic? And I was like Yeeeesss . . . And he was like, It's gone. What do you mean it's gone? I asked and then he starts going on about how he bought his brother's car—which doesn't even fully work—but how his brother could really use the money, and how it'll be good for him to have a project, you know, since

I'm always bagging at the Urology n' Toilet. But I'm just looking at that boat on the vase and how it was so peaceful and I thought about how I could fill up the vase with water up to the boat so it would look like the boat was just rocking on the water, you know? Without a care in the world? And he's going off on mileage and carburetors and things little sailboats don't have or need and he's like a car is better than a boat, anyway. Well, Loomer, a rage came over me. Just this big huge rage, this powerful, dark rage and I just grabbed that vase and I don't know, it didn't shatter over his head like I thought it would. I don't know what kind of glass can withstand a human head, but this one sure did and I mean all I wanted to do was shatter the boat-vase, that's it. I didn't mean to kill him, but the damn thing wouldn't shatter and I kept pummeling his head over and over with it until his head didn't really even look like a head anymore, just a bunch of gooey-brainy slop and the damn boat-vase didn't have so much as a scratch on it and I was so angry that it was still all intact—the boat still looked so peaceful on that vase without me on it—and that just made me angrier so I chucked it at the kitchen wall. And the damn thing broke through the wall! So now it's sitting on my sofa, all perfectly fine, without even a chip. And then there's this ringing in my ears, I think I'm going crazy. But then it turned out to be the telephone. And it was you. And you didn't ask me how I was doing, you didn't seem to care, you had your own journey to plan, and that was fine by me. The fewer questions you'd ask the better. We'd get outta town and just escape it all. No one would really care about Jimmy, he has no next of kin and there'd be no real way to find me so after a year or so of laying low, I could be fine, free, you know? But now this? A double murder? Don't you see? They'll throw me in jail and throw away the key and make you an accessory to both crimes. We have to change our identities. Okay? We're Harpsichord and Ricklobenton Hallmuth of Idaho. We're on the east coast to look for turnips. Our marriage has been rocky but we're working through it. Loomer? Are you with me? Loomer?

Information on this playwright may be found at
www.smithandkraus.com.
Click on the WRITERS tab.

DETAINEE

Sam Graber

Dramatic
Lindsey, forties

*Lindsey is deciding whether or not to torture a U.S. citizen
to stop a domestic school bombing.*

LINDSEY: There's a language to torture. October 2001,
I became a part of that language. The men at the forward operating base knew me as the human poly-
graph, but their word for me was *Piglet*. They said
Piglet, this is *the room*, where you interrogate. We'll
be *down the hall* if your questions bear no jelly. I actually felt sorry for them, tapping electricity to genitals,
cutting, music . . . music, whipping the soles of feet,
more painful than you can imagine. They got pretty
worked up if who they worked over wasn't forthcoming. Then on breaks, calling their loved ones: hey
honey, how's everything back home? Then back for
more *enhanced techniques*. I don't care how tough
you are, or how big the secret you hold, after a week
you'll turn against everything you believe in to make
it stop. You'll try to starve yourself, drown yourself,
but the men bring you back and start again. They call
that rounding. I never went down the hall to see it.
Sound doesn't get out of the room, but it can get in,
and the hallway isn't very long. Well whatever it's
called, I never tortured anyone. But that never stopped
me from wondering, what if I did?

Information on this playwright may be found at
www.smithandkraus.com. *Click on the WRITERS tab.*

Detroit '67

Dominique Morisseau

Seriocomic
Bunny, thirties, African-American

Bunny has come over to visit her friend Chelle, who has just come into some money.

BUNNY: Oooo girl, if I had me any kind of inheritance, I'd see the world. Tellin' you, I'd be in Rome and Paris and all them high n' mighty places with my mink coat and my painted nails and my tea and crumpets—or whatever them folks be havin'. I wanna be just like them White gals we be seein' at the picture show. Sittin' back on one of them satin sofas, fannin' myself and readin' magazines 'til my man come back home from makin' his thousands to scoop me up and lay me right. That's right, honey. 'Cept these niggers 'round here ain't bringing back no kinda thousands. Hell, they ain't even bringin' back no hundreds. 'Less them fools done hit the numbers and picked up a big ol' stack from Sly, only thing they comin' to lay is they hair to the side with that conkaline! That's why I got to do for myself, now. Keep my ear to the ground and tell folks where to get things. Go here for the best hairdo in the city. Go there if you need a new auto part. Go up if you want some good blow. Go down if you want some good bump. Go to the side if you want some down home cookin'. Go crooked if you wanna shoot the dice. Go left if you want the cheapest threads. Go right if you want the finest wine. And go to Twelfth Street if you wanna partaaaaaay . . . . And if you ain't lookin' for none of that, then what the hell you doin' in Detroit?

Information on this playwright may be found at
www.smithandkraus.com.
Click on the WRITERS tab.

Dramatic
Jess, thirty to thirty-five

Jess is sitting in a bar. This is direct address to the audience.

JESS: My mother is dying. My mother is dying, I say it over and over. Waiting to feel something. Nothing comes. So instead of purchasing an economy seat on a budget airline to the south to watch a dying woman who hates me, take sips of oxygen from a nose tube, I'm waiting for someone I haven't met yet. We don't have an appointment. He may not even exist. But here are his stats: One. He is skinny. The kind of skinny that makes people nervous. It's partially genetic; but mostly he just smokes a lot and forgets to eat. I'm so jealous of that. Two. He wears gorgeous clothes. Clothes I've only seen in photos. The kind I could never bring myself to buy. He spends every penny he makes on them. He'd rather be poor than have an unfit garment touch his skin. But he isn't superficial. He just loves himself. Some people do. Three. He looks like my father, who died when I was two, so I can't call upon his face with any precision, but that's probably okay 'cause now I can make my small inventions around the parts I do know such as his body type, his complexion, his hairline. Four. He'll have no qualms about allowing a tipsy degenerate to take him home. Five. We're gonna have some crazy epic drunk sex. Slamming against walls and tearing up bed sheets, et cetera. Someone will probably get a black eye. It'll go on for like, ever. And eventually his particles will become mine and we'll shrink down all microscopic. We'll travel into the corpuscles of strangers, in and out of cells and cilia, through mucous membranes, beneath fingernails, then out into the earth, through the roots of a grass blade, through the hard shells of Amazonian insects, onto the tongues of termites, and oh then we'll get fucking HUGE! We'll billow upwards into the galaxy and cloak the constellations, wrap 'em up like wedding gifts. And then we'll collapse in the pull of our own gravity and reconstitute as a white, heatless star, and wash the universe in our ghostly glow. Yeah, man. That's how rockin' our sex will be. Six. This is more me than him, but he'll fall asleep right after and I'll just stroke him and talk to his sleeping body like people do on TV. I'll tell him this: "I am stroking the space between your ear and your shoulder. I am stroking the space between your hip and your thigh I am stroking the space between your spine and your navel I am consumed with your spaces between." And from these I'll build out my father. Shape him from dust and aromas and smoke and breath and everything else in the invisible world. And later on I'll wonder if I raised my father from the dead just so I could fuck him. Which is pretty dark, right? But first he's gotta walk through that door.

Dramatic
Jess, late thirties—early fortie

Jess talks to her therapist about the de___ ___ow her
eight-year-old son to transition from male to female.

JESS: When we decided to do this, decided to move our family, we wanted to go where Morgan could get the best support possible. Isn't that what you do as a parent? You try to give them the best. So we started out by reading up on who was the best at dealing with this sort of thing and once we found you we moved so we could be close. I mean, it's New York. People here are open-minded right? Luke and I both grew up in a small town, so this is really different for us. Back home there weren't any resources. The school sent us to a psychologist. The pediatrician sent us to an endocrinologist. They did tests. They're doctors. That's what they do. They do tests and hope they can find answers. Some explanation. Was this happening because of something hormonal? Something in his body that wasn't working right. And we went along with it because we didn't know what else to do. Dragging Morgan to doctors and tests, because we were trying to understand what was going on too. We had a little boy who wanted more than anything on earth to be a girl. The only way I could get him to wear boy's tennis shoes instead of girlie sparkle shoes was to paint his toenails pink and pray he never took his shoes off except at home. But all of the tests came back normal. Only the doctors, the spe-

...ts couldn't accept that. In their minds there ...d to be something wrong. And in our minds too, at least at first. I think we were hoping they'd find something. Some explanation. Because then we would know what to say to people. And most of all, we wouldn't have to blame ourselves because there was a whole lot of that going on. The hard part isn't dealing with Morgan. Morgan knows who she is. It was the other people who would ask questions and we didn't have any answers. It's like we didn't have the vocabulary. So finally, I said enough. I wasn't going to continue looking for something to blame for making Morgan who she is. The doctors kept saying they couldn't figure out what was wrong with her. Like if we knew what was wrong it could be fixed. We shifted gears. And that's when we found you. We knew we needed to give Morgan a chance to be her true self. I'm sorry. I'm rambling on and on. It's just that I haven't had a lot of people I can talk to about all of this. It's not really conversation for the carpool line.

Information on this playwright may be found at
www.smithandkraus.com.
Click on the WRITERS tab.

Dramatic
Jess, late thirties to early forties

Jess talks to her therapist about the decision to allow her eight year old son to transition from male to female.

JESS: When we decided to do this, decided to move our family, we wanted to go where Morgan could get the best support possible. Isn't that what you do as a parent? You try to give them the best. So we started out by reading up on who was the best at dealing with this sort of thing and once we found you we moved so we could be close. I mean, it's New York. People here are open-minded right? Luke and I both grew up in a small town, so this is really different for us. Back home there weren't any resources. The school sent us to a psychologist. The pediatrician sent us to an endocrinologist. They did tests. They're doctors. That's what they do. They do tests and hope they can find answers. Some explanation. Was this happening because of something hormonal? Something in his body that wasn't working right. And we went along with it because we didn't know what else to do. Dragging Morgan to doctors and tests, because we were trying to understand what was going on too. We had a little boy who wanted more than anything on earth to be a girl. The only way I could get him to wear boy's tennis shoes instead of girlie sparkle shoes was to paint his toenails pink and pray he never took his shoes off except at home.

But all of the tests came back normal. Only the doctors, the specialists couldn't accept that. In their minds there had to be something wrong. And in our minds too, at least at first. I think we were hoping they'd find something. Some explanation. Because then we would know what to say to people. And most of all, we wouldn't have to blame ourselves because there was a whole lot of that going on. The hard part isn't dealing with Morgan. Morgan knows who she is. It was the other people who would ask questions and we didn't have any answers. It's like we didn't have the vocabulary. So finally, I said enough. I wasn't going to continue looking for something to blame for making Morgan who she is. The doctors kept saying they couldn't figure out what was wrong with her. Like if we knew what was wrong it could be fixed. We shifted gears. And that's when we found you. We knew we needed to give Morgan a chance to be her true self. I'm sorry. I'm rambling on and on. It's just that I haven't had a lot of people I can talk to about all of this. It's not really conversation for the carpool line.

Information on this playwright may be found at
www.smithandkraus.com.
Click on the WRITERS tab.

Seriocomic
Chinadoll, early thirties, Asian

This monologue is a direct address to the audience.
Chinadoll is clueing us into what she must do as an agent,
which is to find "the man," an American operative, her
would-be enemy and lover. The uneaten food speaks to her
state of mind.

CHINADOLL: When you see a beautiful girl alone
in a restaurant, uneaten food in front of her, there
can be many reasons. Perhaps she isn't hungry.
Perhaps the food is bad. But ultimately, there can
only be one *cause*. Fear. Fear that whatever she's
doing will not lead to happiness—the kind of
happiness she's wished for ever since she was a
girl. Yesterday began like any other day. Her mission was simple. Go find the man. He would be
at the Imperial Palace Gardens. The beautiful girl
knew what his goal was. Contact would be made.
Money would change hands. And something would
happen. It was her job to prevent that. So the beautiful girl hid behind a peony bush. Not announc-
ing her presence. Not yet. Just observing. Then,
a Chinese man. A peculiar Chinese man, went up
to the American. They spoke, no more than thirty
seconds, and the man turned and left. It was then
the beautiful girl saw his face. He had a mole.
On his right cheek. A single long strand of hair
sprouted from it. A face not easily forgotten. The
beautiful girl quickly joined the American. But you
know that already. She knew this was going to be

easy. Men are men, and this was no exception. You don't believe me?

Seriocomic
Shirley, mid-teens

*Pointer, Bean Scully's son, has had sex with all six Jel-
lyhouse sisters one of whom, Judy, arrives in the dark of
night with a shoofly pie and, later, some surprising news.*

SHIRLEY: Hello Mrs. Scully. I'm Shirley Judyhouse.
I brought you a shoofly pie, but I think it got struck
by lightning. I'm an awful mess. I'm so sorry. I'm
sorry I barged in on you like this. I just walked two
miles in the flash rain. Figured I'd save some time
by cuttin' through the woods. Them woods was
throwin' fluff last night. Looked like snow was fal-
lin'. But the flash rain's turned it all into a slopyard.
Looks like corn porridge all over the ground. They
say the mudslop's comin'. I made the pie myself.
Three cups of molasses, half a cup of brown sug-
ar, quarter cup of shortenin'. Let it brown slightly
and presto-change-o you got yourself a shoofly
pie. Pointer always tells me how much he likes the
smell of molasses. My Momma says if there's one
way to reach a man it's through your pie. I know it
looks more like a train wreck, but that's 'cause of
the storm. I was runnin' through the woods and all
of the sudden the sky opened up and the flash rain
went white and I heard this *explosion*. Sounded
like a tree snappin' in half. Next thing I know, my
pie's been struck by lightning! Ain't that the crazi-
est thing? I had to pick it up off the ground. I was so
scared I started countin'. My momma always said
that if you count fast enough it'll keep ghosts away.

So I started countin' as fast as I could. I got clear up to five hundred and forty-seven by the time I got to your door. Five-forty-seven . . . Oh my god, there is a man chillin' in the corner and he's bleedin' like a scalped chicken!

(She covers her mouth suddenly.)

Pointer, would you be so kind as to direct me to the whereabouts of the nearest lavatory? I think I'm gonna be sick.

Seriocomic
Shirley, mid-teens

Pointer, Bean Scully's son, has had sex with all six Jel-
lyhouse sisters one of whom, Shirley, has arrived in the
dark of night with a shoofly pie and, later, some surprising
news—she's pregnant/

SHIRLEY: Feel how warm my belly is, Pointer? It's
    like somethin's cookin' in there, ain't it? Missus
    Scully, Pointer and I are lovers of the most dev-
    astatin' degree. And I intend on marryin' him
    and raisin' our baby together. It all starts with a
    little bee buzzin' around a flower, Missus Scully.
    Then the summer breeze just makes things ripe
    and somethin' sweet gets in the air, and fish start
    swimmin' backwards and dogs start howlin, and
    the fire chief. I knew the minute I laid eyes on
    Pointer that we would forge a union of bewilder-
    ing desire and violet passion. He was settin' up in
    a tree on Denorfia Memorial Boulevard and I saw
    that head glowing in the twilight and those long
    skinny legs danglin' over the branches. You coulda
    hit me with a skillet and I wouldn'ta known the dif-
    ference. My momma says that kinda feelin' don't
    come by but once. We been meetin each other near-
    ly every day down by the fishpond, haven't we,
    Pointer? He's told me stuff he ain't never told no
    one. Thoughts that he has. His philosophy on Hip-
    hop Music. How bein' sexy ain't nothin' more than
    a walk and a talk and a way of settin' in a chair.
    He's told me true stories, too. Like about what his

daddy did to him and how he died and how you always go around tellin' folks he fell into a hole. And how you're afraid to go outside. I know about all that, Missus Scully. It don't matter to me. I love Pointer anyways. We pledge our love with johnson grass. And sometimes we go skinny dippin'. And the trout fish swim under our private parts. And sometimes we'll climb up in a tree and eat leaves. One day we ate thirty-four leaves. We fed' em to each other, back and forth. Just like Adam and Eve musta done. That's when we did it. Right on the branch of that tree. That's when we made our baby, ain't it Pointer? And every day I can feel it growin' in me. At first I pitchered it like a baby chick. All blond and soft. Then I started seein' it like a little fluffy kitten. I would sing to it and meow. And sometimes I would pretend like it was meowin' back at me. Then it turned into a puppy with floppy ears. And now it's a baby horse. A tiny one. Smaller than a fist. And soon it'll be a little Pointer in my stomach. With a beautiful vanilla-butterscotch bald head and big baggy basketball shorts. And I'll play classic hip-hop ceedees every night before I go to bed. Jungle Brothers. Black Sheep. De la Soul. Poor Righteous Teachers. And I'll feel my baby's smile ticklin' the inside of my belly. A little Pointer. Even if it's a girl I know it'll come out to be just like Pointer. I'll just name her Pointy.

Dramatic
Gretchen, early twenties

An angry young woman is arrested for murdering the man who raped her. Here, she confronts the prison guard who shows her pity.

GRETCHEN: Yeah I shot him. What'cha gonna do about it, huh? Fucking pig. Fucking woman hating, vaginaphobic son of a bitch! That shithead had it coming. Don't look at me with those sad eyes! Those puppy dogs! Those droopy goopy cellophanes! What'cha gonna do about it huh? Feel sorry for me punk? Fuck you! You goddamn pansy! Momma's boy! Sad sack loony tunes, probably can't even please a woman, can ya?!?

(She leans in seductively)

Probably don't even know what a pussy looks like. Do you? If I showed you mine, would you even know what to do with it?

(She chuckles.)

Yeah, I didn't think so. These bars can't hold me in. These walls can't shackle me. I am transcendental. I am existential! I am anti-matter, ectoplasm, plant destroying phytoplasm. I will melt into the floorboards, delve into the ether, I will eat the ground beneath my feet, and swallow up asbestos. I will rise up on the other side, a thousand times larger than I am right now, and I will cut you while you're sleeping. I will fuck your family, and I will eat your goddamn dog for dinner! That is—assuming that you have one. Do you have a dog there, Mr. Guard?

Mr. Doggy Guard? Or are you just a pussy man like I think you are? *(Pause)* Don't even look at me. Don't even breathe near me. Every particle of air you spew is like a toxin. Every sound you make is . . .

(She spits at him.)

Just get away from me.

(She turns away.)

Why don't you leave me alone? (pause) I did what I had to do. What someone had to do. What my father should have done a million years ago—I put that fucker down. Like the rabid bitch he was.

(She sits.)

Why are you still looking at me? Shit.

(She wipes a tear from her eye.)

Do you want a blow job? Is that . . . ?

(She shrugs.)

Fine. Whatever. Bring it in here, buddy, I'll suck you off. Just like every other guy in the universe. Just blow me and I'll let you live. *(Pause)* Well, what the fuck are you waiting for? I gave you an invitation, didn't I?

Dramatic
Mya, twenties to thirties. African-American

Mya's boyfriend Darrin is a chauffeur for a wealthy man and his daughter. He dreams of one day getting a job in his boss' company as a stockbroker. The daughter is moving, and Mya and Darrin are packing up her stuff. Mya wants to know why the daughter has gotten them a studio apartment in Manhattan.

MYA: We movin' to Manhattan. You and me. Down for each other since two years back. Living in a one bedroom reppin' the Boogie Down. Now . . . a studio in Manhattan. And she's just gonna take care of this? Give us a place to stay in Manhattan while you start your new position? For free. Thing is, most of the 1 don't never see the potential in the 99. We be like there to do all the building and they get to walk through a door or look out a window and never think about what's holding those bricks together. Who put 'em in. Who work late hours. Who got five kids at home and still make sure the floors clean every mornin'. That's the thing . . . they don't never have to see your potential cuz most of us be invisible to them. So what make you visible? What make our short-sighted boss wake up one day and be like—you know what? You shouldn't be no Lincoln car chauffer driving me from firm to firm while I try to convince folks to invest their money with my Daddy. What make her say—you gifted with the numbers and could probably invest folks money much better than I can and I'ma make sure you got a job in my Daddy's company. What make her say—bring yo' woman of two years from the Bronx and take this Manhattan studio 'til you get on yo' feet good? What make her move clear cross the country to get away from you and her Daddy and all of New York? When you just a chauffeur. Driver. Homeboy from the BX that didn't even graduate high school. Got your GED and some econ books and an obsession with math and numbers but no college education. No degrees. No validation card or stamp of approval or golden-seal. Your label is hood. Designer knock-off. And our boss be Armani. Versace. Claiborne. Real deal. What make her see anything in you other than low expectations? Thug. Brute. Hood nigga. Gangsta. Dealer. Jailbird—Just wondering . . . .

Information on this playwright may be found at
www.smithandkraus.com.
Click on the WRITERS tab.

Dramatic
Imen, twenties

The war has been raging for years and Imen is tired. The constant house searches, the soldiers' harassment, her mother's disappearance . . . And now, she just got raped by the next door neighbor who turns out to be her half-brother. As the weight of the recent events threatens to crush her, Imen fantasizes about what death might look like.

IMEN: I see the horses burn. The earth is on fire, the horses are riding at full gallop, black dust saturated with phosphorus bursts from under their hooves, it billows their manes. The red moon crackles under the mares' flanks. I see the horses' entrails fall like garlands over rocks in flames. The entrails hang, like dirty laundry, from the dark balcony of the sea. I see the moon, it vomits blood on the black mares. The last horses hurl themselves into the water, the sea is high. I see the sea rise to meet them, it rises into great towers from which the garlands of entrails hang. The sea rises along with hordes of crows bearing necklaces of horse tongue. I see the crows peck out the horses' eyes, I see them burst the eyes with their beaks. I see the crows dig into the mares' guts, they tear out foetuses which they spin like balls on the tips of their beaks. The crows shake their wings heavy with the horses' blood. The blood rises, rises up in the air, the black wings fall back over the waves and the blood rises up in the air. I see the blood spiral up, it gathers dust from the stars, gathers the cries of children, the cries of horses, the cry of the sea, it becomes a sphere, it becomes a comet. The sphere swells, it swells and it rises, it's very high in the sky, it reaches the moon, it knocks down the moon, it takes its place, the place of the moon. Up there, the horses' blood coagulates. I hear the horses' blood burst into laughter.

Information on this playwright may be found at
www.smithandkraus.com.
Click on the WRITERS tab.

Dramatic
Nina, Forty

Nina is watching her kid play. She has struck up a conversation with a father who's there watching his kid too.

NINA: I mean, look at what's happening out there. Civilization is totally breaking down. Everyone's just yelling at each other. Or ignoring each other—plugged into whatever it is that isn't really happening. And all this . . . media. Facebook and Instagram and Pinterest. All these narcissistic declarations instead of conversations. I mean. Stores have blogs. What's a store going to say to me that's meaningful? And meanwhile the planet is just . . . shuddering. Just swelling and sweltering and flooding and storming and we all just go deeper into our screens—flatter. We just get more and more . . . flat. Tuning it all out with anti-depressants. And blaming our psychic fatigue on gluten. Everyone thinks they're allergic to gluten. And of course, I know some people really are, and the wheat has been genetically modified into, like, cardboard, and God knows it's not easy to digest, but I think for most people the exhaustion, and the bloating, is just from denying reality every day. The end. The decline. Of everything. The decay. The toxins. You can't even tell people they need to read about what's in their meat, their milk—the chemicals and the bleach and the fecal matter—they're feeding their kids. Everyone's so obsessed with protein, they just say "I can't." I don't want to know!" I don't

---

want to know? What kind of existence is that? I don't want to know.

Dramatic
Cari, Ten

Cari is tagging along to the Starbucks and the spa with her mom. She's geeky. She doesn't have a lot of friends. She's full of knowledge and excited which she doesn't usually get to express. She is talking to the audience, though this is probably more than she speaks to any of her classmates all day at school.

CARI: I want to be a veterinarian at a zoo so that I can touch all the animals, even the large predators, well, ok, especially the large predators. I mean, I'm pretty sure that when zoo veterinarians perform surgery on tigers and polar bears, they take a few minutes to rub their bellies, tickle their paws, maybe even kiss them on the nose while they're sedated. I also want to be a musician, probably the clarinet because you can play all kinds of music with the clarinet: classical, jazz, blues, folk. It doesn't have genre limitations like the saxophone or the harpsichord. I would like to go on record as saying that the harpsichord is my favorite instrument. I think it's what it would sound like if spiders played music on their webs. I also want to be an astronaut unless they start letting regular people go into space—for way less money, and a trapezist. The circus performers on trapezes? But really, I should become an inventor because then I wouldn't be limited to one field. I could clone tigers so that they would never be extinct, and create musical instruments that you can hear in outer space, and invent an air freshener-type-device that emits a chemical that makes people nicer. And then have it installed in every classroom in every school in the world. And the Senate. They already make something like that for dogs.

Information on this playwright may be found at
www.smithandkraus.com.
Click on the WRITERS tab.

Dramatic
Andie, thirty-five

Andie is a barista at Starbucks (one of the settings of this play) and a bystander in a controversy about a local billboard for a spa. The billboard is of a beautiful woman with arrows pointing at various "problems" and suggesting "solutions" that the spa offers. The controversy has caused Andie to reflect upon her own relationship with her weight, her image, and her future. She is speaking to the audience.

ANDIE: I hate having my picture taken. I avoid looking at myself. I know I'm fat. But I also know that this world I live in—this white, American world—equates extra pounds with ugliness and inadequacy. And that is a perception, not a truth. Some days I dream of being black or Latina; part of some culture where I can pull off the sexy fat-girl thing. I don't dream of being thin. Not anymore. I tried for a long time to manage my weight, and I can't do it. I don't know how, so I don't bother dreaming about it. Changing my skin color, my ethnicity, my cultural identity, feels more plausible than losing a significant amount of weight. And honestly, I would just like to be part of a group that accepts me, like this, and finds me beautiful. My friends have said, you can meet someone on-line. And I've tried that. I've met people. And you know what? They're right. There are plenty of people out there willing to have sex with a big girl. And be really excited about it too. But they don't want to take you home to meet their mama. Sometimes I think it's my personal purgatory to have to work in this place where everyone is so thin and perfect. Well, not everyone. But it *feels* like everyone. Every few days I catch a soccer mom looking at me, a big, bleached-white, toothy smile pops up to hide her judgment. And I know she's thinking, "I'm so glad I'm not fat. I'm so glad I'm not you." And I just want to say, "I'm so glad I don't have that fucking BRAT pulling on my pants asking me for another fucking cookie!" But that's not true. I like kids. Not most of the kids here. But the kids *I* would have, I would like them. *(2 beats)* Except I'm not going to have kids. I tell people I don't want them, because it's worse to have them feel sorry for me, better they think I don't want what everyone else has. But the fact is, I can't even get a date. I'm 35 years old and I can't get a date. So how am I going to get married and have kids?

Information on this playwright may be found at
www.smithandkraus.com.
Click on the WRITERS tab.

2015 THE BEST WOMEN'S STAGE MONOLOGUES

Dramatic
Gloria, thirties

*Gloria is sitting alone on a bench late at night, hoping to
be a serial killer's next victim when she is approached by
a man who might be the killer.*

GLORIA: The Slasher. I understand this is a favorite
haunt of his. You know who I mean, that serial killer who's been in the news lately? He's done some
really interesting work. Totally disembowels his
victims. I'm here to meet him. Hopefully. Are you
the Slasher? The Slasher is brilliant. His work will
be studied for years. There's no question. He's got
a real technique. I intend on being his next victim.
Oh, yes. I've read everything about him and I've
grown to admire his work. How he makes a small
incision at the jugular first, then ties his victims'
hands behind their back and disembowels them as
they writhe. The paper said he uses rope but I'm
afraid that'll chaff my wrists so I brought a latex
tie.
        (She pulls it out of her purse.)
And I went to Super Cuts for a new do and the
Clinique counter for a facial. I hope he doesn't
mind leaving me face up or seated, seated would
be better. I'd like the pictures to look good. I realize I'll never get to see them, so whatever happens,
happens, I guess I'll have to be okay with it. I just
thought it would be nice, for the newspapers and
books and all, to at least be pretty in death. *(Pause.)*
So how do you want to do this? Is there a posi-

tion you want me to get into? Or . . . ? You are the Slasher, aren't you?

Information on this playwright may be found at
www.smithandkraus.com.
Click on the WRITERS tab.

Seriocomic
Brittany, late twenties

*Late at night in a university town Brittany, a confused
and very disturbed young woman, looking for the Crisis
Center, mistakenly knocks on the door of Ben, a writer at
a writer's workshop at the university. She is troubled by a
number of things, most recently because she believes that
impulses from her brain are causing a lamp post on campus to go out every time she passes it. She is really upset
about her own life, but has displaced a good deal of her
anger onto the writer's workshop, which she has come to
see as evil. She is probably not aware of how insulting her
tirade is to him.*

BRITTANY: That damned writer's workshop draws
every self-obsessed loser in the universe to this
place. You want to talk about people who have an
irrational view of their own personal significance?
What a bunch of neurotic gas bags. I used to work
in the library, and while I was supposed to be
shelving books I was up in the stacks reading these
thesis novels from the fiction workshop. What a
bunch of shit. They're all the same. Safe little sen-
sitive precious pieces of minimalist self-referential
bullshit, with maybe a little wry twist at the end, so
subtle it's hardly even there. God. Hasn't anybody
got any balls around here? This bland shit is supposed to be literature? It's hardly even writing. And
then you all sit around and congratulate each other
while secretly hating each other's guts and then
go out and hire each other to teach the same sort
of crap to other mediocre losers like yourself. It's

like a black hole that swallows up talent and shits mediocrity. God forbid anything here should ever have any fucking deep personal significance. God forbid anything could actually mean anything. Oh, no. Let's call it apophenia or delusional reference or slap some other damned stupid label on it so we don't have to think about it any more. Because if the universe actually meant anything, it might mean that the fucking writer's workshop is just one big giant shit factory.

Seriocomic
Brittany, late twenties

*Late at night in a university town Brittany, a confused and
very disturbed young woman, looking for the Crisis Center,
mistakenly knocks on the door of Ben, a writer at a writer's
workshop at the university. She is troubled by a number
of things, most recently because she believes that impulses
from her brain are causing a lamp post on campus to go
out every time she passes it. She is really upset about her
own life, but has displaced a good deal of her anger onto
the writer's workshop, which she has come to see as evil.
Ben has been suggesting to her that her lamp post experience is just her presuming a cause and effect relationship
that doesn't exist. But she rejects his reductionist attitude,
making her case for intuition and imagination over logic,
and comes back once again to her fixation on the workshop, which she resents because in her view it demands a
mindless following of stupid rules and an elimination of
imaginative creation.*

BRITTANY: But how do you know for sure? Just
because nobody has figured out an experiment
they can repeat over and over again and make
the same thing happen, like dropping a bowling
ball off a bell tower or something, doesn't mean
there isn't any connection. All kinds of things
are connected that we don't know about. That's
what science is. And that's what art is, too, right?
Making connections between things that other
people didn't make before. Which is why your
stupid writer's workshop stories really, really
suck the big one. Because they're not making
connections that other people haven't made before.

They're only making connections that other people have already made. Somebody is going along and sneering at anybody who does anything different and making them stop, and the result is a drab, dead, lifeless, worthless slop. It's dead. And you're dead. All of you people are dead. You think you're creating something but you're not creating anything. Nothing is being created here and nothing of any value is being learned. Because it's all just the scared mediocre puke of scared mediocre people. And meanwhile, all around us, there's this whole universe of unexplained and terrifying things that all of you are too damned full of yourselves to even acknowledge the possibility of. And it's people like you who run the world. Mediocrities. People with skills just a little above average end up running everything, because that's what they're good at. They don't make anything. They don't create anything of any real value. They just like telling people what to do and feeling superior to anybody who actually uses their brain.

Dramatic
The Wife, forties

Lasso of Truth concerns the origins of the character Wonder Woman, and the unusual home life of her creator. Here, The Wife discusses balancing love, marriage, and career in 1930's America.

THE WIFE: Behind every great extra-marital affair . . . is a woman. Who keeps the household running, keeps showing up at her job, keeps the bills paid. Loves a man who is a dreamy wanderer, and gets what she paid for: a home, a family. A sanctuary away from the chattering nonsense that is so much of the world. But not here. Here it is quiet. One can think. I have no fears of walking in the man's world, progressing up the corporate ladder under the noses of and despite the shocked surprise of my so-called *Superiors*—every one of them inferior to me in every way—I rather enjoy the wrangle and the jab, the competition, the being damn good at what I do. I am damn good at what I do. But I must have some quiet when I get home. I must have a man who is not afraid of me. A man who lets me stand my full height. In my own home, I need to let all this go. He can do what he likes (so long as he's respectful of me, discreet). I'm not so interested in all that. He can do what he likes, as long as he is *here* with me. In our quiet home. Where I can come home after a long, hard day at the office, kick off my shoes and have him curl up at my feet, head in my lap. Tell me what he's dreaming today. He will do something extraordinary, I know. Something he would never have been able to do without this. Our home. Our life. No one else *has* to understand. It's enough that we do.

Dramatic
Beverly Long, forty-three, African-American

Beverly Long, Ed.D. is a mother, educator and the Interim Principal of the high-performing Millburn High School in well-to-do Millburn, NJ. Having abandoned her high-powered position in the troubled Newark, NJ school district just a year prior, she had hoped for smooth sailing as interim principal. But after the after-school shooting of a student, exposed postmortem for being fraudulently enrolled, she is facing an onslaught of concerned citizens and parents who blame her for jeopardizing the safety of their children by enrolling a child associated with such fatal violence. In this speech she tells Denitra, an African American parent who Beverly feels is perhaps the only person she can speak honestly with during this turmoil, about the irony of her situation.

BEVERLY: Have you ever spent some time in a Newark high school? Part of my job was to walk through every school in the district to observe teachers. Elementary and middle schools were generally fine. Jordan went to Hawthorne Elementary. Excellent school. But high school? Something shifts. I remember being on a walk through in Jordan's high school, the bell rings to switch classes and out pour the students. And it's the usual thing, but this day something was . . . I don't know I was just more aware . . . The conversations amongst the kids were just—n-word this. B-word that. F-this. Right in front of adults. They didn't care. I heard a teacher in the distance shout, "Get yo' a-word to class." And this was them on their best behavior, I mean, they knew we were coming to walk through. Lots of lingering. Lots of on-the-corner loitering. A security officer a little too friendly with one of the little girls for my taste. Then I think to myself, he's not but twenty years old. He most likely graduated from there two years ago. There were lots of kids, an innumerable amount, not carrying anything at all, which means they had no books no homework to turn in, nothing with which to take notes or carry handouts or store materials they received, no paper and pen even. And this was not because they all had laptops or tablets or anything, like the students here. The bell rings for class to start, passing is over, but no one's in a rush. Just shuffling along. I decide sneak away from the walk to peak in on Jordan's class—I kept him out of the general population. He was in "honors academy," I made sure. And I never tell him when I'm going to pop up, so he'll always be on his best. and I get to his class and what do I see? . . . All the boys are lined up on one side of the room, girls on the other, facing the wall, spread eagle while two security officers wand them down. Another walks through the aisles of the class looking through their bags . . . for contraband. The teacher's entering grades, and I tell her who I am and I ask her, "What's going on here?" Figuring there was a serious incident of violence. But she casually says, "Random security check." They pick a classroom at random every morning. Like numbers out of a hat. They got my baby on the wall doin' the pat down perp walk—he's done nothing wrong, and what killed me was that this was normal. All of it— the hallways, the cursing, the low expectations, the loitering—The kids were used to it. I had become used to it. The teacher was used to interrupting her lesson for random security checks. I mean, this was a classroom—supposed to be a learning space, a safe space, but there they were spread eagle . . . and not at all bothered by it . . . laughing even. And I realized: My son was being indoctrinated into *prison* culture because of my career aspirations. I pulled him from that school that same day and quit the next. Just packed my stuff up, and walked away. Right in the middle of curriculum approval. I didn't even finish presenting to the board. I didn't want to be associated with that mayhem, not one more minute.

Information on this playwright may be found at
www.smithandkraus.com.
Click on the WRITERS tab.

Dramatic
Denitra Morgan, thirty-eight, African-American

Denitra Morgan is a determined 38-year-old mother, community college graduate, and an LVN at an urgent care center. After being exposed during a school enrollment audit, Denitra is confronted by the principal at her Newark apartment for lying about her home address to enroll her daughter at Millburn High. Though they are not friends, they are connected and certainly committed to ensuring the successful matriculation of Denitra's daughter through the school. After being asked by the principal, "What were you thinking?" with respect to the lying, Denitra uses her personal experience in this speech to counter Beverly's implications that her actions were anything less than honorable and necessary to secure her daughter's future.

DENITRA: Where'd you go to high school? I bet you were one of those special Negros they plucked from the hood concrete to refine. I bet you were a part of some pet integration program where they bused you out to some white suburban bliss— You think you're better than me, Beverly? With your three degrees? You think I didn't work hard enough? You think I don't deserve—? *(beat)* I was damn near the top of my high school class. Right here in this same neighborhood. I was a cheerleader. Volleyball. In youth and government. I did everything by the book. I thought I was going to Harvard! I couldn't figure out how I was the best thing since sliced bread at my school, but I couldn't break a thousand on the SATs. How I was acing three AP classes my senior year, but couldn't pass the national AP tests. Why, when I'm forced to settle for Essex county college, they have me in remedial math and English. How can you graduate high school and need remedial anything? I couldn't even register for some of the classes in my major 'cause I didn't meet those academic standards. I spent two years in remedial. Embarrassed 'cause I told everyone I was going to Harvard to be a lawyer! And look at me! Look at me! "What was I thinking?" I was thinking I didn't want that for Noelle. I want her to *know* that she meets the *highest* standards. I wanted her to be able to go to a top four-year institution where they prepare kids to be the leaders of this world. Not the people who take your order. That's what I was thinking. And I'm sorry. I'm sorry you got caught up. It was not my intention. But I was not thinking about you.

Information on this playwright may be found at
www.smithandkraus.com.
Click on the WRITERS tab.

Dramatic
Sula, twenties, Haitian

Sula is speaking to Joel. Joel has just expressed his love for her. Sula has feelings for him, but cannot allow herself to act on her feelings. She has come to America to escape her dark past with her newborn son Toussaint. This is the first revelation of her past.

SULA: You've heard stories of Houngans? Some are born into it. I was. My mom was a houngan. She died when I was three years old. She's nothing but a voice on grainy cassette strings, a scent from an old bottle of perfume. The features of her face, I don't remember, but her beauty I do. I can still see it. It's the kind of beauty myths are made of. A beauty that connects you to the deities, that make you a perfect houngan. My great great aunt said she was cursed with it. Said I'm cursed with it. Many men wanted my mom and many men had her. They came from all over searching not just for legs to rest between, but for somewhere to purge all their unwanted memories. Their wives and girlfriends couldn't endure it, but my mom she could. She welcomed it. I was born from one of those men. My father was the worst and she loved him the most. He emptied himself in her daily. She died from carrying him inside of her. My aunt feared that I would have the same longing and for a while I fought it. But then I met Toussaint's father, a man who tortures the president's political opponents until they agree to disappear or die. A man so bitter and broken, he cried during sex. He fought his battles inside of my body and it made me feel whole. I would have done anything for him. Including calling the spirits, the deities, allowing them to possess my body and give him the instructions, the magic to torture people. If it weren't for Toussaint, I'd still be there, with him, doing that. So you see I'm not who you wish I were. I'm not pure and I'm not good.

Dramatic
Birdie, eighteen

Birdie Combs is talking to Pinky Walker, an 18-year-old chunky male dressed as a glamour girl in tight dress and stiletto heels for Halloween. They are in a sparsely furnished room in a nursing room. Birdie is there to visit her grandmother. When the grandmother called Birdie "a bitch," Birdie choked her. Pinky, an aide, has walked in and called the cops. Pinky and Birdie wait for the cops to arrive.

BIRDIE: And then she looks right at me and calls me a "bitch." I come here every week to visit her and she calls me a—? I mean, it's just, I didn't need that. Don't go to parties anymore. Go to school every day. And after that I'm working cash register in the grocery store. Counting change for tight asses who, I love this, who throw those dumb magazines in their cart at the last minute, sorta cover 'em up, like they're too good to read *National Enquirer.* Everybody reads crap. You know how I get my kicks? I squeeze lemons and make the sourest lemon-aid I can, so sour it's hard to drink. But I drink it. And I put Tabasco sauce in my coffee. Never see my old friends any more. There's so much I . . . avoid. And she calls me a bitch. I think you're the bitch. You're the high-maintenance bitch. With your nails and painted face and hair and tight-ass way you dress. I used to dress like you. Dress like I was having fun. Not anymore.

Dramatic

Maritza, twenty-eight

Maritza is with Liliana, with whom she has just had sex. Liliana is trapped in an abusive marriage to a very wealthy man, and Maritza pleads with her to leave him and come back to Chicago with her.

MARITZA: You're going up with me, I'm taking you back with me. Let's make this happen. Let's do this. We do it before he comes back. We do it in a way that we can't get tracked. We drive, ok? We drive all the way up. Borrow a car from my cousin. I won't tell him just so he doesn't—Yeah we won't tell him and we dismantle that narco truck of yours. And that way Fabi doesn't get it either. Just do away with it. Trade it with my cousin for parts so he can give us some hooptie that will take us north. You leave that iPhone here. We get you a new phone. You take only what you need. Ok, you take whatever you want. Whatever we can fit in the back seat and in the trunk. Nothing electronic tough, ok? No iPad. No laptop. No . . . whatever else you got. Just you and your drawers and your face paint and your fancy shoes. But come on, not all of them, ok? And we go Liliana and we start. We just start it. Take the video out of pause and we start it. Like it was meant to be. This is a long time coming. Every so often we keep getting pulled back for a reason. That's why you called me, Lili. And we are going to be fucked up unless we finally do this, we're never going to be whole. We'll walk around with big gaping holes for the rest of our lives.

(beat)

Please baby, you have to leave with me.

(beat)

Tonight.

Dramatic
Yuya, forty-five

Yuya, the housekeeper, pleads with Liliana not to leave her husband, Alberto, even though he is very abusive, to run off with a former girlfriend with whom she has reconnected.

YUYA: How many years and I've kept my mouth shut? Not one word. And don't think I don't know the *cochinadas* you do with her. Doing disgusting things with your bodies—the two of you. *Sucias*. Liliana, you know you can't leave with her. What, you would leave your father, the way he is right now? So sick? You would leave your *pobre mamacita*? That poor woman. You think you get to run off with that *puta* in your happily ever after and not think about anyone but yourself? *Mi'ja*, what will happen to your family, then? You know Alberto will cut them all off. You can't go anywhere. Too many of us depend on you. Who knows how long this guy will keep you around but in the meantime, you have to be a smart girl *y aprovechar*. (quick beat) Man, if I had your possibilities, I would not be fucking this up. I'd be saving every penny I could. Hiding shit. Stashing it away. You need to get smarter about this, Lili. And then, when it's done, then maybe you can think of . . . maybe you can think of whatever *cochinadas* you want to think about. When you've squeezed everything you can out of this whole thing. *Es un* investment. Are you listening to me? This is all an investment. But you gotta buck up. Be a *mujercita*. You think I don't want to go off, gallivanting and . . . I don't know. You think I like being for your every whim? I didn't say when I was a baby girl, a *mira*, that's what I want to do with my life. Live at the whims of those who have more. But I got people who are counting on me and I'm the only thing they got. And your *Papi* and your *Mami, tu hermana* Cecilia, you're the only thing they got. It's not about you, it's about them. So buck up. You listening? You're gonna have to buck the fuck up.

Dramatic

Liliana, twenty to twenty-eight

Liliana is married to wealthy man who abuses her. She has called her old friend and former lover Maritza to come down from Chicago where she lives, but Liliana isn't sure what she wants from her. She only knows that she's desperate.

LILIANA: Mari, you think I'm here . . . you think this doesn't cost me. You think it's just nothing. That you're nothing to me. To me you're actually . . .
> *(beat)*

But everything costs. This is something I realized very early on. Everything has a price. And these two days with you, they're going to cost me big. But I don't care, I'll pay. Because it was so worth it. He is a monster. He likes choking. He likes belts.* He likes sticking things in places where they shouldn't be stuck. He's not a human to me sometimes. When he's grunting on top of me, or when he's ripping out my ass with no warning— because with Alberto, the more I scream the hotter he gets. But only if I mean it. No faking that shit . . . And that's the price. I pay for everything I own, Maritza. Everything I have. That car out there? Oh, I paid for that. With interest! Please, stop being in a fucking Antonio Banderas movie! Just. Stop. If you say something. If you do something, what will happen? He tosses me and my father's medical bills don't get paid. My mother loses her house, her health insurance too. My little sister has

to come back from college and what? Wait tables?
And me. I mean, what would happen to me? I have
nothing. All I have is him.

Dramatic
Fabiola, twenty-five

Fabiola is supposed to be in college, paid for by her wealthy father. She tells her stepmother, Liliana, that she has in fact dropped out and, as a result, her father has cut her off.

FABIOLA: He saw that I wasn't going to school. I haven't . . . I'm not in school right now. I just needed some time to figure some stuff out. But that's only because I didn't enroll, ok? And the thing he doesn't see is that I made that decision with like a clear adult mind. It wasn't like my first two years where I had to drop out of classes because I wasn't going, you know? Because I overslept or because, well, most of my professors were total douche bags. They didn't know what the hell they were talking about. Whatever. That's not even the . . . But why can't he see that this time, I made a conscious, responsible decision. To actually not waste money and time and whateveraggravation. I consciously didn't enroll this semester. Alright, I didn't enroll this whole year. Ok? I didn't enroll this year and well . . . He got all- Oh, god he scared the fuck out of me. He was like King Kong. You know how he gets like King Kong. He never gets like that with me. And he just . . . took it all away. He's never done that, Liliana. I'm like really scared right now because he's never done that. Even when I went to rehab for the . . . I mean he was like more caring than he was mad. Oh, my God I'm going to kill myself. That's what I'm going to tell him. That I'm going to kill myself. You have to talk to him.

(beat)

Liliana. You have to talk to him for me. You have to help me! I mean, what am I going to do? Live here like a prisoner? Like a slave? Just because he got into a mood?

MINE

Laura Marks

Dramatic
Amy, twenties

Mari is a new mother, but ever since she gave birth she's thought that something is wrong. She becomes convinced that the baby she gave birth to is not the baby she now has. Here, a young woman named Amy reveals to her the horrifying truth.

AMY: I can't stay long. So I need you to listen: The night your daughter was born, some of us came into your room, and we took her, and left one of ours in her place. That's the part that's hard to explain, because . . . your language is seriously lacking in sophistication; if I say "fairy" you think of *My Little Pony* or something like—How can I explain this? We feed off of you—don't look at me like that; it's not "you," just your by-products. You drink cow's milk and eat eggs, don't you? We don't have many children; at least, not anymore—and when we do, our offspring are weak; they need a human infusion. So a few hundred years ago, we realized that our best chance of survival was to swap one of ours for one of yours. A changeling. And most of the time, you never know the difference. You might have a little feeling that something's not right, but you devise some explanation. Now obviously, when we do this, we'd like to get the fairy child back someday. But it's not easy. We watch them for years, waiting for our chance, until one day a child you thought was human disappears, and you never find out why. And as for the human baby, in the past, I admit, we had . . . disposal methods, which got a little ugly. But it's all different now: nowadays we like to keep the human child, and raise it. Because we've learned that it's good for us to study you; it helps us imitate you. And it's working: we get a little more like you each year. And I suppose, once you've given up your own child to be wet-nursed by a human, a human child is . . . something to hold. Better than nothing. *(Pause)* I wasn't supposed to come back. But I wanted to see her, so I did. And now we have a problem.

Dramatic
Eleanor, twenties

Eleanor, the daughter of Karl Marx, is playing Nora in the London premiere of Ibsen's A Dollhouse. She has been asked by Friedrich Engels to address a group of his followers.

Eleanor: Thank you, Mr. Engels! I must admit it feels odd to address you as such, when most often it's as Uncle Engels that I refer to you, so close are you to my father's heart. So close are you to mine. And so close are you to the heart of our cause. That which is the cause of all working people who seek justice. I have just come from the theatre where I–as well as some of my comrades— were employed in a playing of Henrik Ibsen's *A Dollhouse*. No doubt, you've heard rumor of the scandalous plot, and I assure you every whispered lambaste is true. But I urge you to judge for yourselves. Mr. Ibsen's play concerns the very topic on which I am bound to touch this evening, the matter of "holding women in common," as the capitalists have so accused us. Indeed, such an idea is possible only in a state of society that looks upon woman as a commodity, a thing to be "held" by another person. Today, alas, woman has only too often to sell her womanhood for bread, as if she were a product. But to the socialist, a woman is a human being—*imagine!*—and can no more be "held" in common than a socialistic society could recognize slavery. Furthermore, I ask you, who are these sup-

---

posed virtuous men who speak of our wanting to hold women in common? I tell you, they are the very men who own and sell your wives and sisters and daughters. Have you ever reflected, you workingmen, that the very riches you work to place in the pockets of the bourgeoisie are used to debauch your own sisters and daughters, even your little children? They are robbing the worker to rape his family. And so we *must* cry out, "No! A woman is *not* property! A woman is a human being! And as such, she cannot be held by *anyone*!"

Information on this playwright may be found at
www.smithandkraus.com.
Click on the WRITERS tab.

Dramatic
Eleanor, twenties

Eleanor, the daughter of Karl Marx, is addressing an audience of workers in Chicago.

ELEANOR: Ladies and Gentlemen—strong working class citizens of Chicago, though I may be foreign to you, believe me we are all brothers and sisters. We are a family united by work. Your capitalists will tell you that socialists want to do away with family. Truly we don't want what is called family by today's standards. For today your families are crushed beneath the unbearable weight of slavery. In your own city, you find men who are millionaires and women who have to choose between starvation and prostitution. I have also been told by your capitalists that you in America enjoy such freedom that socialism is not needed. Well, from what I've read in your own newspapers, all you seem to enjoy is being shot by Pinkertons. I'll be quite raw. You working classes of America have no more freedom than with us. Men who toil from morn to night are *not* free. Women who slave in factories to make those very articles they cannot afford to buy are *not* free. Children who labor at the mills when they should be at school or at play are *not* free. Brothers and sisters, you have your 'social question' here as anywhere else. America is *not* Free! And so what is to be done? We must form unions. Hold together and your victory is certain. The votes of New York, Philadelphia, and other cities in sympathy offer proof that your victory has already begun. It began with the 68,000 votes for the socialist party in New York, and the 25,000 votes given here today. And don't forget that to those votes you've got to add 68,000 and 25,000 votes more for the *women* who cannot vote! And when you men and women have once understood what your rights are and have determined to have them, such wonderful things will happen that you will scarcely believe. What can the few thousands of the exploiting class do to suppress the millions of workers, when once we *will* to be free? Work with us, brothers and sisters. Work with us, *work with us* and freedom *must* be ours! For *"Freedom's battle once begun / Bequeathed from bleeding Sire to Son / Though baffled oft, is ever won!"*

Information on this playwright may be found at
www.smithandkraus.com.
Click on the WRITERS tab.

Dramatic
Katharine, sixties

Katharine's only child, Andre, died of AIDS. Now, twenty years later, she has arrived at the home of Andre's lover, Cal, who is now married to Will. She tells her about Andre, and about her life.

KATHARINE: I'm the only one who thought Andre was a difficult child. He was smarter than anyone else. He had secrets. I was afraid of him. He could be so remote. I didn't know where he'd go in his head. I wanted him to take me with him—away from Dallas and a husband I didn't love and never *tried* to love, he was unlovable. Some people are, you know—I've turned into one—but I would have married anyone who took me out of Port Chester, even if it was only across the railroad tracks to Rye. But Mr. Gerard wanted to go west, young man. Which is ridiculous because he wasn't a young man and Dallas isn't the west, it's Dallas. I was, I am a Yankee. I remain one. I need four seasons. I need to be around people who know what time it is. I don't suffer fools. I was a smart young woman. I thought I was going to die with that secret. My father worked in the post office. My mother spent the day ironing and baking and cleaning and we ate on a table covered with an oil cloth. With my Port Chester High diploma, I went to work for a dentist, Dr. Minnerly. Dr. Pain his patients called him. He didn't believe in Novocain. I hated him and I hated my job (you can tell your husband I know how much I use that word; he didn't score any points there). Every week I saved my money until I had enough to buy myself an evening dress that would get me into the Rye Country Club Spring Dance where I knew I would meet my savior and I did. I got him to marry me like *that*.

(She snaps her fingers.)

And I didn't get knocked up to get him to do it, like most of my girlfriends. I turned on the charm. I can when I want to. I've given you a glimpse of it. And I always had good legs. I still do. Andre got his legs from me. He had beautiful legs for a man. And I thought I could be happy for a little bit. I don't know what I mean by happy anymore. I thought I did then: content, not jealous, able to stop jiggling. I'm a nervous woman. I still can't cross my legs without jiggling them. Andre once said, "Mom, you look like a woman in heat when you pump your legs like that." He could be very fresh. I wanted to slap him. Then, out of the blue, just like that, he decides he wants to be an actor. Drama club, acting lessons, singing, dancing. And I was his chauffeur for all of this. I read a lot of good books in the car, waiting for Andre, our grey dachshund happily drooling away on the seat beside me. I got thanks, I got presents, I got "I love you" but I didn't get him. I got everything else but him. He was supposed to let me love him the way I'd never been loved. I was going to make him happy the way I'd never been. And then he was off to New York City. Suddenly he had a life and it had nothing to do with me. All I was was Andre's mother: the woman who bore him. He wrote something when he wasn't much older than your boy. "God bless the Lord. God bless my mommy. She has good things in her oven." I was Andre's mother to him as much as I was to any of his little friends. "Can I have a cookie, Andre's mother?" "You can if you call me Mrs. Gerard." But they never did. I wasn't a person to them either. I was Andre's mother. I got pregnant when Andre was four. I aborted it. I never told anyone. I was waiting for the right time to tell Andre. It was going to be our final secret together.

Information on this playwright may be found at
www.smithandkraus.com.
Click on the WRITERS tab.

Dramatic
Daweti, late twenties early thirties, black
South African

Daweti lives in a shack in Soweto. She is dying of AIDS. Her male friend Thabo has come to see if he can do anything for her. He has expressed fear about what he will do when she dies.

DAWETI: It is custom that if a person is killed in an accident or something tragic. That the mourners come to that site where they died, and take a branch from some special tree . . . umm . . . You are Zulu, you now the tree I'm talking about. They put that branch over their shoulder and use it to guide that person's spirit home. But there is one condition Thabo. You can't look back. The mourners can't look back because if they do that person's spirit can get lost forever. When there is nobody left to remember you that is when you have truly died. You will put a piece of aloe in water to remove bad luck. You wait a week and do not socialize, wear all black and shave your hair . . . well you're good there. After that week of mourning you forget about me. Don't keep me here. And when your hair grows back like a flower in the springtime . . . or when it should have grown back like a flower in the . . . anyway. You will be new and should start over. And if you ever feel my spirit gently tugging you back, you tell me and I will go away from your memories. You will be happy. You will be free.

Dramatic
Daweti, late twenties-early thirties, black
South African

Daweti, a high-educated woman, is living in a shack in Soweto, where she is dying of AIDS. This is direct address to the audience.

Daweti: You know, I have such beautiful dreams now. When I first found out I was sick my dreams were scary, and terrifying. Of bad things happening. I would trip, or robbed, or shot and I would jolt awake like, *(inhale, she opens her eyes)* and I couldn't go back to sleep. One time I was crying in my sleep. I had lost something, I can't remember what, but it was important, something I didn't know was important yet. I couldn't recognize what it was but it felt like a piece of me being ripped away, and I wasn't whole anymore. When I woke I had tears leaking out of my closed eyes. My pillow was wet, not from drool. I would drool so much, my poor sister and I had to share a bed growing up, she would call it Lake Daweti. *Last night I took a swim in Lake Daweti*, she would say. I would laugh. Life was . . . Anyway . . . The day I told my mother that I was sick. I came home from graduation and she was so happy. She greeted me in the front yard and gave me a big hug. I gave her my degree and it just came out. I couldn't hold it in, I was sick. And she changed right there in front of me, something behind her eyes shifted, like a bird flying away behind her body and my mother flew away on the back of that bird. The whole time standing there, in front of me, where a minute felt like a life time . . . Gone. And as she turned around and walked away, she never looked behind her, left me standing in the yard. And when she locked the front door I knew that I no longer had a mother. And . . . I . . . Ever since then my dreams are magical, beautiful, effervescent. Sometimes I try to stay asleep all day to keep living in them. Ha, I love it!

Dramatic
Anna, thirties

Time: early twentieth century. Anna Akhmatova, beautiful Russian poet, is hit on the head by a brick during the Nazi bombing of Leningrad and seeks shelter in an old basement which turns out to be the site of the famous Stray Dog Café, where all the famous Russian writers, artists and dancers gathered before the Revolution. There she meets once again many of her now dead friends, and finds herself reliving some of her past experiences, including this moment, perhaps from her thirties, in which she tries to explain to a friend why she has had such a deeply troubled and turbulent love life.

ANNA: Clearly all men are insane. Men I've just been introduced to hold my hand and tell me they want to marry me. I don't trust them and I don't like them. I fall in love with the worst of them instinctively. And they're always trying to kill each other. It's a pity they aren't better at it. But I create my own unhappiness. My loves are designed by some lunatic in my head to self-destruct and generate the maximum amount of pain conceivable. Even when I'm throwing myself into something completely there's somebody in my head who's already withdrawing. I pretend not to love but do, or I pretend to love but doubt so strongly that I sabotage what could be happiness and gravitate like a sleepwalker towards despair. I'm drawn to what's hopeless and ignore what's possible. I have scripted an unhappy life for myself, those who love me and those I love, but for what purpose? So I can write poems about it? I enter into each new love as into a house of mirrors, with the dim awareness of betrayal to come. I don't want to be a reflection in somebody else's mirror.

Seriocomic
Anna, fifty-one

Anna Akhmatova, beautiful Russian poet, is hit on the head by a brick during the Nazi bombing of Leningrad and seeks shelter in an old basement which turns out to be the site of the famous Stray Dog Café, where all the famous Russian writers, artists and dancers gathered before the Revolution. Here, near the beginning of the play, she is explaining to her friend why the cellar they have stumbled into and the people she knew there have meant so much to her.

ANNA: The best times I had in my life were at the Stray Dog. There was a gate you went through to come down those steps like descending into Hell. It was always thick with smoke and mystery and laughter and sex, and it seemed to exist so vividly in the present, but there was a timeless feeling here, as if you'd stepped into a vortex in which past and future coexisted. If you looked closely at the walls at four in the morning you could see the birds moving and the leaves rustling before dawn. This place is the center of the universe. At least it seemed that way to us. At night, when I drift off to sleep, I return to this place. I have come down those narrow steps so many times, through the doorway so low Stanislavsky had to take off his head to get through. Artists and poets and actors and dancers. They blocked up the windows to keep out the real world and painted harlequins and birds on the walls. It was Bohemian paradise. Everybody slept with everybody, and we told ourselves it was all right because we were different. We were artists. There were no rules for us. An extraordinary collection of drunkards and sluts who all thought we were geniuses, and some of us were right, but how unhappy we made each other. And yet I have missed it so desperately. There was just that little stage there, but on stage or off, everybody was always performing. Somebody would play and Tamara would dance. She was so beautiful. Such a delicate creature, but strong. Dancers are surprisingly strong. And the only virgin in the place. They took bets on who would defile her.

Dramatic
Woman, thirties to forties

*In this monologue, the character is simply called Woman;
she's in her 30s-40s; she is addressing the audience and
speaking to her world record of dating the most men. It's
a play in which characters hold world records in every-
day things, like dating and never growing up and watching
sunsets, etc.*

WOMAN: When you get to be my age, you stop believing in certain things, the way in childhood
you stop believing in myths and stories, in magic.
You stop believing in the things you were taught
would happen if you waited long enough—that
you'd find love, and a satisfying thing to do every day, that there was always still time to become
happy, to find a new routine. So when I met Mario,
I had given up. I was playing chess every afternoon in the park; I was seeing the game from so
many different angles, a new one each day. I was
a lawyer. I hated my job. David had just left me
and my heart was broken for the fifty-ninth time.
I was only thirty-one. I already had the record.
There was nothing to prove anymore. I turned to
chess. This would be black and white. And, I mean,
in chess if you lose, you just lose, you don't go
home and sob and tear up photographs and reread
awful novels that make you feel worse and reread
letters and listen to mix tapes. With chess, you just
lose. So yeah, when I met Mario, I didn't even con-
sider him. I mean, I thought I was done with all

that. I thought I could choose to be done. I didn't realize that our lives repeat themselves like songs on mix tapes that go on forever.

Information on this playwright may be found at
www.smithandkraus.com.
Click on the WRITERS tab.

Dramatic
Polly, thirties

Polly has reconnected with her step-brother Graham, who she hasn't seen in years, at their father's funeral, and they have begun a love affair. She is talking to a friend about her affair.

POLLY: Have you noticed that very conservative people cheating on their very conservative spouses seem to go in for this very messy "I'm breaking all the rules kind of transgressive talk dirty to me" sex? Not that I know a lot about these things; I'm just saying. Okay, and plus, there was this whole quasi-incest factor even though we're not related—and that made it— you know, that was—And of course, his father had just—died. NO. I'm not going to see him again. Oh come on. What good is it to be single and liberated if you can't go back to the lame-ass Midwestern town you ran away from once and sleep with your married ex stepbrother? In a car. And sometimes, and I know you know this, sometimes we are able to see into the heart of another person, into their very innermost secreted heart, and touch them there and set something into motion, and, why not? Why not do that when we can? Why not? I've never mentioned him before? Oh. He's the son of my mom's second husband, the mean drunk one. Right. Him. No, I am not going to see him again. I mean, Mundelein? What the hell is that? Libertyville? What the hell is that? I am not going to see him again. No, no, no, no, no.

Dramatic
Cat, seventeen

Cat's father, Graham, has begun a love affair with his step-sister, Polly, with whom he reconnected at their father's funeral after not seeing her for many years. Cat is determined to do something about it.

CAT: I work very hard. I get A's in all of my classes. I am on time for everything. For everything. I work harder than the boys but I don't get rewarded. I hear there was this thing a long time ago called "The Revolution" but my mom doesn't seem to know about it. My mom is always exhausted. Church doesn't help. My mom is on a lot of committees and medication. I think my mom wants my dad to come home. My dad went to see his ex-stepsister in New York and he never came back. I don't know what he's doing there. I mean, ex-stepsister? That's not even a real relation. Plus, she's like, she's not, you know, she's not a Christian. I think she must lead a very scandalous and potentially exciting life even if it does not fall under the contract or rubric or whatever of the Church of God. I went on the Internet this morning and looked up this Polly Freed. I know a lot about her. I am going to get my father back. I am going to bring him home. Mom's in the bedroom with the lights out again and everything's quiet and sometimes, you just have to take matters into your own hands. Do you know what I mean? The Amtrak is an amazing way to travel. All Aboard. You see the country, really you do. I don't have my own car, and air travel is expensive and also, lately, uncomfortable and dangerous. But this feels just fine. On the train. In the Club Car. Meeting people and listening to them talk. I could listen to people talk all day. Really, I could. And they have these stories, and they are. Dying. To talk. To tell you things. Everyone. So this is good. I arrive tomorrow. And in the meantime, big windows, strangers, the Oreos and seltzer I brought from home, and the way the land keeps changing. This is amazing. The way it changes. Have you ever just watched it change? Next stop . . . next stop.. next stop . . . And he'll be waiting for me. My dad. He just needs someone to tell him where he lives.

Dramatic
Cora, thirty-seven, bi-racial African-American

*Cora has travelled with father to Liberia in wartime to
visit the graves of her father's parents. They have been arrested by a Liberian official who thinks they are spies. She
realizes they are in deep trouble and is trying to talk her
way out of her situation.*

CORA: I'm the one who supposedly took the picture
of the skyline, even though I didn't do it, because
I don't care about your stinking skyline. But, fine,
if you want to think I did it. Fine. I took a picture
of the skyline. You win. You already won twenty
years ago. Don't you realize that? You won. We
lost. I mean, this is how it turned out. But, if you're
happy, I'm happy. If you think this country's doing well. Great. Wonderful. Wonderful. My father
lost everything, Sir. Land, money, status. Everything. And let me tell you something, and you listen to me very carefully because I don't like how
you're talking to me. You have no right to talk to
me like this. In spite of everything, that old man,
my father, loves this country. He cares about it.
He's proud of it. He wanted to come because he's
old, and he wanted me to come with him and I
didn›t want to, but they forced me to because I'm
the eldest. Nobody wants to come to Liberia. Nobody in the world. Nobody. It's embarrassing to be
from Liberia. But my father tells everyone. Proud-
ly. Even though you killed his brother. My uncle
is buried in a pit, and nobody will tell us where.

And that›s the second reason my father came, to try to find out where his brother is buried. But the phones don't work and everyone is dead or they left, so he couldn't find anything out. But the main thing he wanted to do, and it took me two weeks to find out, is that he just wants to visit his parent's grave. Is that so threatening to you, Sir? I›m tired of this. I'm so tired of all of it.

(beginning to cry, but stopping herself)

I just want to go home, Sir. Please, I just want to go home. I'm really sorry for everything. I'm sorry I was rude. And I'm sorry I took a picture of the skyline and I'm sorry I attacked the soldier.

Information on this playwright may be found at
www.smithandkraus.com.
Click on the WRITERS tab.

Seriocomic
Jessie, twenty-four

*In the year 1926, Jessie Armitage, a young woman of 24,
is sitting one night with her best friend, Jimmy Casey, 29,
at their favorite spot, overlooking Grim Lake, in a small
town in east Ohio. Jessie is beautiful, smart, funny, tender,
spirited, a wonderful girl it's easy to fall in love with, and
Jimmy has been deeply in love with her for many years.
She will kiss him, go swimming naked with him, and cud-
dle with him, but she won't be his girl, and she's warned
him never to expect her to. Her secret is that she is hope-
lessly in love with her brother John Rose, an actor who is
now making silent movies in Hollywood. She is missing
her brother very much, and waiting for him to send for
her, but he never does, and she is noticing here that Jimmy,
frustrated and angry, is starting to suspect the truth.*

JESSIE: I don't know why my brother makes such terrible movies. He's such a great actor. He played
Hamlet with Mr McDuffy's Shakespeare company
all over the world. And now he's in Hollywood
making these awful movies. I don't know what's
the matter with him. I've seen this one maybe seven
or eight times. That's the big advantage of working
at the Odessa Theatre. After I sell the popcorn and
take the tickets I get to see my brother's movies
over and over again. Of course, the downside is,
the movies are dreadful, and I've got to listen to
old Mrs. Dooley play the piano. After hearing you
play, and then going over there and listening to her,
it isn't even like she's playing the piano so much
as trying to beat it to death. I love it when you play

the piano. I could sit and listen to you forever. I wish I had the patience to learn how to play. I'll never live long enough to sound as good as you. I love that one piece so much—that one Chopin étude. Maybe you could teach me to play just well enough to play that one. Except probably I won't be here. I'm going out to Hollywood to see Johnny pretty soon. I think he needs somebody to be out there with him. I know he's drinking too much. I can tell from looking at his movies. His eyes. I can always tell from his eyes. We have a special bond. I can tell when he's really unhappy. I could help take care of him and then maybe begin my career as an actress. I know I could do it better than most of those girls. What's the matter, Jimmy? You've been looking at me so strange lately, like you just saw a ghost or something. That's what the people in the movies are like. They're like ghosts, playing out these stories in the dark. Movies are like memory and actors are ghosts. Don't you think?

Seriocomic
Maia, forty to sixty

Maia is an extremely intelligent woman who speaks with angels—on the cusp of becoming an eccentric. Maia is speaking to her psychologist. She is frustrated about her apparent eccentricity, which embarrasses her. She speaks to "light beings" or angels if you will. She wants to use this gift to help people, but it just confirms her fear of being an eccentric.

MAIA: They're good company. The angels, that is. I'm never bored. "Oh, so you knew President Kennedy? My goodness, you hung out with Charles Dickens?" They started showing up when I was in third grade. I kept getting thrown out of class. "But Mrs. Orlowsky, she was touching your desk and you said no one could touch your desk." And they thought about putting me in a mental institution, but I was ferociously smart so they skipped me into the fourth grade instead. So I guess their thinking was—"I think she's insane, but let's put her into a really fraught situation and see what happens." And there in room 201 on the same floor as the big 4th, 5th, and 6th graders of Public School 18, I was automatically labeled a freak just for being skipped. And I didn't help matters. At recess I used to chase the angels. The other kids just watched in horror. Oh, and also I used to draw on myself with markers. That's kind of odd, right? I wasn't very popular. And then there was Mr. Densmore. He had a mustache. I think I was in love with him. And I'm a lesbian. Explain that. Of course I didn't know I was a dyke until I was married. That's also when the angels started speaking—well not really speaking but letting me know what they were saying. Do you think my lesbianism is tied to my angel visits? Is this what I'm supposed to be talking about? There are three here right now by the way. I know it's not about you, but I'm wondering who Ellen is. Sorry. I do that. I think maybe I'm not particularly comfortable talking about myself. Ellen says she never blamed you. It's not that I think I'm crazy. Although I do wonder. I mean, look at me. I have read the DSM over and over and can't find the particular delusion or pathology which I exhibit. I don't mean the angels—they are simply fact. I mean my me-ness. It's really really sad. They're not sad. Not really happy either. They just are. You know. Content. Do you know what color sadness is? It's blue. They were right when they called it the blues. Indigo almost. When I mentioned Ellen just now—not to keep coming back to you—your aura went dark blue—almost black then grew pink—now pink can mean just about anything. Ellen is smiling I think. See? It's slippery. I keep wanting to take the focus off of me. So . . . me. I'm sad. Duh. If I could see my aura, which I can't—not even in a mirror—and I have spent a lot of time in front of mirrors—I suspect my aura would be a rainbow of blues. Everyone is in so much pain and the angels never are. But you can't convince people that dying is not the end. I try. I fail. Ellen is nodding by the way. Kinda nodding—I sense that she's agreeing with me. She's lovely. People think they are paying me to communicate with those they lost, but they're not. They're paying me to convince them that we live on.

Dramatic
Jaclyn, forties-fifties, African-American

*Jaclyn works in a doctor's office. She has become more
than a little "difficult" and is, in fact, on the verge of being
fired. During this monologue, delivered to her co-worker
Ilene, who is white, we learn a lot about the cause of the
huge chip on Jaclyn's shoulder.*

JACLYN: I made the strangest discovery on the Chicago
Avenue bus today. It was really a kind of flashing illu-
mination, you know, the kind of light that draws you
in and brings everything closer, so close you can almost see the molecules working together. You know
what I mean? You know, I take that bus every day.
I get up, I catch my straight-to-the-point Chicago
Avenue bus which ends up here—almost to the
door. So close in fact that I sometimes pretend that
I've just been dropped off by my chauffeur. And
each and every day on the Chicago Avenue bus,
I end up standing back-to-back with these young
professional types, young white men—sometimes
four or five of them—all of them from the same
beautiful housing development on May Street and
it's a weird mix, you know. There's these four or
five professional types riding a bus crowded with
a lot of people coming in from the west side: the
hotel maids, the bellhops, the clerks at Macy's,
the Ontario Street post office, the receptionists at
Northwestern Hospital, the janitors, the janitoress-
es. And I hear these pretty men, these pretty white
men talking about Rasheeda this and Rasheeda that

and I'm thinking to myself: who in the world are they talking about? Who is this Rasheeda? But then today I was jostled by the crowd into the inner circle of these four to five white men, when the bus stops and this large, stern, frozen face middle-aged black woman pushes by them and gets off, and one of these young professionals turns to the other and says "there goes Rasheeda." And I thought: they know her? How do they know her? They can't know her, can they? But then there's another stop and this time, three middle aged black women get off, pushing their way to the exit door and one of those young, flushed pink-skinned professionals turns to the group and says: There must be a Rasheeda convention and they all laugh so loud it fills the bus and the seats and the ears of everybody near them with hot air and I thought: Oh, I get it. Rasheeda is their name for all middle aged black women who work the hotels, the post offices, the department stores, the doctors' offices and as the bus pulled up to my stop, I thought: oh my, my, my. Do they think I'm a Rasheeda? Do they want to take revenge against me as one more Rasheeda in the world who at some time during the day, for a few seconds, a brief few minutes might have control of something they want—a stamp, a clean towel, an appointment with the doctor? And as the straight-to-the-point Chicago Avenue bus approaches my stop, I try hard to keep them from thinking that about me. I hold back my feelings. I steel myself into a rigid, frozen-face model of exactness but I still get so nervous about getting off the bus that I almost miss my stop because I don't want to get off and hear them call me a Rasheeda. It's a Muslim name after all. My name is Jaclyn. Jackie, if they want, if they insist. But that's nothing like Rasheeda. But the bus stops and I do, I do get off and I hear all five of them say in unison: "Rasheeda Number 5! That's a record!" And they laugh, you know, because it's very funny, Very, Very funny and so Clever of them, of those young white professional men who ride the bus together and together have found a very specific and lovely sounding, secret code of a replacement for the word nigger. So 21st Century, I think. Don't you? Using a secret code to set off laugh bombs on the bus and then chuckling under their breath at their victims who wonder if ignoring the problem only makes it worse and who then wonder if setting off a bomb, a real bomb, might clear up the problem. You know, like them Muslims do, like those Islamic people. Boom, boom. Kill, kill.

Dramatic
Lois, sixty, African-American

Lois is failing in her efforts to get her family to sign up to be a part of a class action lawsuit against the state of Oklahoma for the role they played in the devastating Tulsa race riot of 1921. In this scene Lois speaks to her son Seth's girlfriend Debbie, the one ally she has in the matter, about why the lawsuit is so important to her.

LOIS: It was for school. In middle school, Anna took it upon herself to have him tested and he tested off the charts. Genius level. She got him an offer to go to the private school where she teaches. School out by them. At the time I was livin' all over. Nothin' solid. His father had left. He couldn't find work. Ashamed he couldn't provide. I was probably harder on him than I should've been. It wasn't all his fault. But he left. And it was hard. So when Anna offered to take Seth in, I thought it would be good. The stability. He would ride with her every day, I'd take him on weekends. But to get work, I had to work weekends so months would go by, you know? And she had all these opportunities for him in the summer. She always offered to pay, 'cause I couldn't afford . . . I only meant it to be temporary, but next thing you know, he in high school. Got into Briarwood— I couldn't afford no Briarwood, neither. But they offered—well, I suspect it was really Anna, but they offered. And Seth said he liked it. And I didn't want to uproot him, just 'cause my heart was broke, you know? He was doin' so good and gettin' exposure to things, places I ain't know nothin' 'bout. Spent every Christmas together though. But one year he call me, day before I'm supposed to get him from the bus, he say, "Mama, what you think 'bout comin' to Chuck and Anna's for Christmas? They got a extra room." I said, "Hell naw!" That was the one time during the year it was just me and him, you know? But he got home that year and moped around so, that I spent my last on 2 bus tickets to drive us back up. Been spending Christmas here ever since. Hurt my feelings, but it hurt my feelings more to see him lookin' so disappointed, you know? To know my child wasn't happy bein' with me. I just want to see him smile. Get what he deserve. That's why I'm on this lawsuit. 'Cause he deserve that. Imagine where he may have been had that not happened? Had me and his father been able to build on what my grandaddy and his daddy before him, and the one before him had built? How far would we be? What I would have had? I wouldn't have had to . . . . Who we could have been? But Seth ain't tryin' to hear that though. It's like . . . something . . . turned his ears, his heart from me. But this here lawsuit is right. I'ma get this. Chuck is gon' sign that affidavit whether he want to or not, and we gon' get this.

Ronan Noone

Dramatic
Lisa, thirty-eight

Lisa has been married for 11 years to Tony (Toe). She is talking to her longtime single friend, Gasper about his playboy behavior and how much she would enjoy a night without any marital or family responsibilities.

LISA: Do you know what I would like? Will I tell you what I would like? I would like to live, just for one day, like you. I would. I would. No husband or child and don't get me wrong I love them both dearly, the child more than the husband, which is natural, but don't tell anyone that, I mean it's natural, but you just don't tell anyone, especially Toe, not because it would matter I mean he knows I love him dearly, but you don't want to confirm that you love your child more than him, even though anyway, anyway what was I saying I was saying, yes, that I would like to be like you for a day, you know, no responsibilities, except work and then, you know what I would do, I would come home and open a bottle of wine and drink it all without worrying that my child thinks I drink too much, I might go out and flirt with some guy just to confirm I'm still really attractive without worrying that my husband might go crazy if I did that. Of course I wouldn't sleep with him coz that just feels nasty, I mean I have a fantasy but I just wouldn't go that far which is kinda sad considering it's a fantasy which means I'm censoring my fantasies which kinda defeats the whole idea of fantasy. And then I'd come home and eat apple pie a la mode without worrying I was going to get fat. I guess my point is that's what I imagine it's like to live in your shoes for a day.

Information on this playwright may be found at
www.smithandkraus.com.
Click on the WRITERS tab.

Dramatic
Janice, thirty-eight

Janice is talking to Sylvie, her co-worker who cannot conceive a child. Janice has five children and is trying to weigh up her feelings of guilt about being so fertile, about wishing for time alone, and thinking about a time when she came first.

JANICE: You can't think further than the pregnancy. You've got no bloody idea what it's like. I'm in a permanent state of anxiety, worrying if they're healthy. Are they being bullied. Will they bully. Why aren't Matilda's legs straight. Will it affect her self-esteem. Will she get a boyfriend. Is Lee *ever* going to make a friend. I didn't know did I? I mean you get them over one stage and there's another bloody stage to take its place. And always in the back of my mind, how are they going to turn out, how will *I* make them turn out. Will they be selfish bastards, will they fit into society or not contribute to it in any way whatsoever. So I need to get away, resent them even. God, why am I justifying this? It's not like I'm not thinking of them constantly, about things that are there, and everything that's not. The weight of responsibility is overwhelming. **I am nothing *but* a mother . . .** If Jim wasn't there to remind me who I used to be I'd wonder if the old Janice ever existed . . . I find myself imagining how he'd cope if I left. I wouldn't, but if *I'm* thinking that, what's *he* thinking? D'you know, I'm half way through a book I started in two thousand and ten!

Information on this playwright may be found at
www.smithandkraus.com. *Click on the WRITERS tab.*

Dramatic

Lily, sixty-five

Lily's husband has just died and she has gone into work to tell everyone and because she needs to make some sort of connection. She does not blame her husband *entirely,* for the state of their marriage but the realization that he knew how unhappy she was has shaken her. Now she is questioning why she accepted such mediocrity and is confessing to herself and to her colleagues about her inability to be loving to him, even at the end.

LILY: I never said it, I never said anything. He was afraid an'all. I'd never seen him afraid before. We had bloody hours alone together without a single distraction. No telly for him, no kitchen for me. He said, "we've had an alright marriage haven't we Lil?" I evaded the question. "At least we went the distance not like most, fake laugh. I still didn't say anything. You weren't too unhappy were you?" . . . I ask you! That meant he knew, the bastard. I wanted to say, "You've had years to ask me that, it's too late *now*, you pillock." What *was* that. Conscience? Fear? God I hated him in that moment. I think he wanted me to take his hand, comfort him, I should have, I know that, I know I should have but I didn't, I couldn't. I was the same with him as I've always been. Don't get me wrong, I *used* to want something more, in the early years. I would have liked a *bit* of romance or something bordering on loving but neither of us knew how to get it. And after thirty six years of, whatever it was we had, you can't just conjure up affection. I didn't feel any. I wanted to feed the ducks if you must know, escape. There was just too much emotion . . . I did feel sorry for him, but only in the way you feel for a dog that's been mistreated. I thought, why is it you lying there, needy, dying and wanting *something else* from me. Why isn't it the other way round? But if it had been me lay dying, I don't think I would have wanted him anywhere near me.

Information on this playwright may be found at
www.smithandkraus.com.
Click on the WRITERS tab.

Dramatic
Sylvia, fifties

Sylvia, an English professor, has a Ph.D. candidate named Emmi who started out wanting to do her dissertation on an obscure female horror fiction writer and now wants to edit an edition of her collected works, in order to rescue her from obscurity. Here, Sylvia talks about self-esteem workshops she did with young women.

SYLVIA: What makes you feel good about yourself as a woman? Without much thought, some shiny, clever young thing would raise her hand and say "when a boy tells you you're pretty." Every time. Every school. Every gathering of girls no matter how large or small. And the psychologist would say, yes, very good, and what else? And that would be the defining moment of most of these girls' lives, because in all the workshops I ever attended—more than twenty—that question was answered by silence. By a long, profound silence in which of a group of disparate girls—nerds, cheerleaders, stoners, goths—experienced, collectively, a bear-trap closing on them. A silence where they each realized nothing else made them feel like a woman. When we asked the same question about what makes a boy feel like a man, there was a flurry of answers—women, cars, sports, achievement, bravery—the list went on and on. That is what it means to feel like a man. But to feel like a woman? If we pressed them, maybe answers would surface like baking, dressing well, having a nicely decorated house, but they rang hollow and sounded demeaning, even to fourteen-year-olds. And their eyes would meet, and girls who had hated one another the class before—cheerleaders who had looked at math nerds with contempt as they walked into the room, would find a painful sisterhood in the absence of satisfying answers. What makes you feel like a woman? Gives you a sense of how narrow our definition really is, doesn't it? I finally stopped doing the damned things. All our *self-esteem* workshop was accomplishing was to show them what a one-legged stool their self-esteem was balanced on, and they already knew that. So we would tell them "you need to learn to define yourself in ways more like the ways you define men." That line actually came out of my mouth. And we wonder why that's the age we lose girls. And they carve the word bitch into their arms with razor blades. And the little girl who used to laugh and bounce with purpose and creativity and enthusiasm, disappears for a long time. While boys are exploring wonderful ways of blossoming into men with women and cars and honor and football, these girls don't exist beneath their skin. Except for brief flashes when a boy tells them they are pretty. Or when a razor blade reminds them they exist for an equally brief flash.

Dramatic
Julie, twenty

Julie is at an S & M sex party but has come into the kitchen to get away from the scene, where she has met John, who is hanging out there, having a smoke. He is an intern for a famous photographer who expects him to be at his beck and call 24/7. It's her first time at one of these parties, whereas he often frequents them. It turns out, she's the daughter of his boss. He's a "dom;" she is more of a submissive—but here, she lays into him, puncturing his illusions about himself.

JULIE: How fucking old are you? No, seriously, really. Who the fuck do you think you're going to be at thirty-one? You're going to take me to Detroit? Me and Kristen are, what, we're going to hang out in Michigan and be some kind of little harem for you? We're going to live in, what, some fucking box on the waterfront, so you can be even more fucking irrelevant than you are now? Seriously, John. Who the fuck do you think you are? Do you think you're going to be my dad? *(Pause)* You think you're going to be my dad. You think you're going to be Geoffrey fucking Bradford, you're going to have all the shows, you think, what, Eli Broad's going to want you hanging on the wall? Leonard Stern? Do you know what my dad was doing when he was thirty-one? Yeah, of course you know. And he got divorced from my mom, because he was fucking a nineteen year-old fashion model. What does Kristen do? I bet she's a barista. *(Beat)* I don't think he even remembers all their names, you know? There are just so many. So, yeah, that's what my dad was doing when he was thirty-one. You know what he wasn't fucking doing? He wasn't taking phone calls in the middle of the night with his pants down and then running off like somebody's fucking lapdog to do God knows what stupid thing because he didn't have the nerve to tell someone to fuck off! That's what he wasn't doing. You know what? This is why you're nobody. This is why—what do you think is going to happen for you? You're like, oh, I want to be this, I want to be that, but you're not fucking anybody. *(Beat)* My dad is somebody. He's always been somebody. Everyone fucking hates him and he doesn't care. He just does the work he wants to do and everybody else just tries to fucking keep up. And he's always been like that. He wanted to be an artist so he just fucking went and did it. And he has one intern after another come in and follow him around and beg for his approval and he doesn't fucking care, because none of you, none of you guys are going to do work that's worth shit, because if you were you wouldn't fucking bother to work for him. *(Beat)* Don't you think if you were actually talented somebody would've noticed by now?

Information on this playwright may be found at
www.smithandkraus.com.
Click on the WRITERS tab.

Dramatic
Casey, thirty

Casey, a Marine, has come home from a tour of duty in Iraq, where she was raped. She is severely traumatized by that, and by something she did, as she tells her husband, Kevin. Sean is their 10 year-old son.

CASEY:
(stating this very simply, without emotion)
I shot a little boy. I thought he was about Sean's age, he was probably older. He was in the village we always passed soon after we'd leave the base. He'd wave, I'd wave back. He'd yell for us to throw him candy, pens, money, food. I started putting life savers in baggies with pennies like it was Halloween and throw them out to him when we rolled past. He started calling me Madonna, I have no idea why. I asked him his name. He was in the market and I asked him his name and he smiled up at me, with this toothy grin, "S'aheed." He was just this funny kid acting goofy on the side of the road. Like Sean, he was a goofball. And I started looking for him every time we passed. The others in my unit, knew him, said he was the son of an insurgent. Not to get friendly. They used them as decoys, to set you up for an ambush. Don't be fooled. They aren't normal kids. Don't think of them as kids. Think of them as the enemy. As soon as I got there, everything that could go wrong did. And then that last convoy, Kellerman was spooked, he really should've stayed back, he was driving erratic, he

was gonna get us killed I thought, so I took over, I took the wheel and I started driving, Kellerman was on the radio. And the boy, S'aheed shows up in the road, he must've dodged in between vehicles at the last minute. There he is right in front of me. I swerve not to hit him, BOOM, there goes Kellerman. On the next mission, I saw the boy on an overpass.

(first time she pauses)

He had something in his hand, he was dropping it. I don't know what it was. Could have been a grenade. Could have been a rock. Could have been a Snickers bar. I keep going over it in my head. When did I decide to lift my rifle, when did I aim, when did I pull the trigger. I don't remember thinking about it, or feeling one way or another about it. Took two shots. I missed the first time and then I hit the target. I aimed my weapon at a little boy and took him out. I was doing my job. The one time I didn't fuck it up in their opinion.

Information on this playwright may be found at
www.smithandkraus.com.
Click on the WRITERS tab.

Dramatic
Ali, eighteen

In a small town in North Carolina, 18-year-old Ali lives with her older sister Evelyn in a house that has seen better days. Their middle sister Lexie has just returned from a five-year tour of duty in a recent war. In this scene, Ali confronts Evelyn about their shared past.

ALI: You go round all high and mighty, but when Lexie shipped out, I remember you prayin' to all the saints in heaven that she stay there a long time. Wanted her gone. Far, far away, 'cuz you hated she always did better than you. She'd win some prize at school? You'd be all weirded-out. She made a real decision with her life? You didn't know what to do with. 'Cuz she's just like Daddy. Lexie is just like Daddy and Daddy was a piece of shit. Piece of shit for leavin' us, piece of shit 'cuz Momma got sick after he left, piece of shit it was his fault she up and died, 'cuz if he hadn't left, maybe she wouldn't have gotten sick in the first place. And Lexie got his eyes and Lexie got his spirit and Lexie a soldier too, and that just puts you out like hellfire. But you know what? Lexie's more than you. Come Day of Judgment? Book gonna show she done right. And you, with all the powerful decency you say you got— Nobody's gonna remember you. Nobody's gonna say "Oh that Evelyn, she's a golden child." Your name drop in the bucket? Good riddance. That's what people will say. Nobody but nobody's gonna sing at your grave.

Dramatic

Lexie, twenty-three

In a small town in North Carolina, three sisters live in a house that has seen better days. Lexie, the middle sister, has just returned from a five-year tour of duty in a recent war. In this scene, she confronts her older sister Evelyn.

LEXIE: Think I wanted to go over there to the stink n' shit? Think I had some kinda choice? I'm a grunt. Plain and simple. Bitch ho dyke grunt from no-where. That's what they called me, called all of us.

(as a sergeant's order)

Bitch ho dyke, get down, and give me ten.

(as an Army cadence:)

Bitch ho dyke from ol' town Sodom, strike match-es on her bottom. Or you think just 'cuz Daddy served, they'd give me special privilege? Daddy was a grunt too. I talk to Barry cuz yeah, he's easy. We drink. Shoot the shit. Doesn't ask me about anythin'. And I don't ask him 'bout what he does or how many kids he got from all the different women he's had. It's simple. I want simple now . . . . Not that that's somethin' you'd understand. 'Cuz you want close and in your face and oh let's be out here and think about how good everythin' is in this country. You ACT like you got rage and fierceness inside you. You tear into Ali, 'cuz she's so easy to tear into—She's a baby doll she's that easy—and you twist that knife, and you make her twist it too, until both of you are sayin' things you shouldn't be sayin' over some JOB that ain't even out there, and ain't ever gonna be out there ever again. And here I am, right in the thick of it, right in the four-feet-down-in-the-ground head-throbbin' mess of it, and all you care 'bout is whether I stay for supper? Supper gonna make everythin' go away, Evelyn? Supper gonna heal like some preacher at church? Oh mighty the ground we walk on when we profess our healin' to an earth that can't listen no more, 'cuz it is busted-up and weary and sick-fast and hungry.

Dramatic

Lexie, twenty-three

In a small town in North Carolina, three sisters scrape by a meager existence. Lexie, the middle sister, has just returned from serving in a recent war. She suffers from PTSD. In this monologue, she describes to her older sister Evelyn what it feels like to be back home.

LEXIE: Think I sleep? Sleep and sleep all through the day? I never sleep. There is no shut-eye to speak of. I lie in that bed up there in the house under that fuckin' ceilin' full of water stains, and I stare. Hard. Thinkin' of nothin' and everythin'. And when you're all hushed or pretendin' to be, I slip out, yeah. Not for a goddamn "escapade." No, ma'am. I run, past the dogwoods and the mess of snakes and the heat that gathers in the old barns, and I find some spot somewhere that feels lost and stinky and beat to shit, and I hide in a muscle of water all night, sweatin', shiverin' and full of shame. So, don't you be tellin' me what you think I'm doin' or not doin', or how I should be behavin' to help you feel better about the goddamn mess we're ALL in here, there, and everywhere anyone calls home. Light shines in the distance, but what I see ain't no light. No, ma'am. What I see's fire, pure achin', and it's gonna rage all over this here earth, until we got nothin' but to hold on hard close, and hope we ain't ash before mornin'.

Dramatic
Bibi, thirties

Bibi is a mousy and dull woman who has realized that she figures prominently in an intergalactic alien war.

BIBI: When I was a little girl I this recurring dream that my father and I were building a greenhouse in the back yard. We just worked and worked, around the clock. And then when the little greenhouse was finally built we filled it with little pots of dirt. And little, like, jars of water? Shelf after shelf of them. And when we were done we watched television. Something with Tom Selleck in it. And then sleep hit me like a tidal wave and my dad carried me to bed and tucked me in. And I slept for a thousand million years. Literally. When I woke up my dad was long dead. Just a skeleton. So was my mom and the cat and all the kids at school. I was still in my nightie, but very, very old. I had a long beard like Rip Van Winkle. I went out into the backyard and there was the greenhouse, but covered in moss and ivy now. Still, it was standing after all those eons. A kind of testament to the ingenuity of the human race. So I opened the door and it was all, "CREEEEEEAAAAK." And I couldn't believe what I saw —life had developed in the pots and jars. But not normal life. Whatever we'd planted had morphed and reproduced and morphed again until it was something completely different. New plants and strange fish with gaping mouths and lights for eyes. A weird bird flew over my head all, "KAW KAW." And I just stood there, amazed. Because I had made that. Me and my dad. And only a little bit on purpose: we'd only meant to grow rosemary.

Information on this playwright may be found at
www.smithandkraus.com.
Click on the WRITERS tab.

Dramatic

Nancy, fifties

Nancy has just found out that her son David was raped when he was seven years by the son of their long time friends and neighbor. She confronts the rapist's parents to warn them of the dangers of their son.

NANCY: First, I want to say that this isn't easy, and I ask that you please let me finish what I need to tell you without interrupting or asking questions. I promise you, for the sake of your grandchildren, you need to listen until I am finished speaking. In the fall of 1978, in your home, when our family came over for dinner, your son violently raped David. Your son led David downstairs to the basement to play, then began intimidating my son by wielding nunchuks and a sword. He made David remove his pants, then held the blade to my son's face. We spoke to David in person and he confirmed what happened. I urge you to speak to your son as soon as possible before he can do any more damage. Your grandchildren may be at risk. I know we've been friends a long time and I sincerely feel sorry for you both. Robert and I both hope you have wonderful lives but we ask that you never attempt to contact any of us ever again. Do not call or write us, no Christmas cards. Nothing. I only hope that your son eventually gets caught, and that he spends the rest of his life getting raped in prison.

Dramatic
Edda, fifty plus

The year is 1920. The place is Vienna. Edda is speaking to her employer and now friend, Heléna Altman, for whom she has served as housekeeper for many years. Heléna's husband, long thought killed during WW1, had in fact deserted. He has now returned to claim his wife and take her with him to Rotterdam. Edda has been doing her best to help Heléna prepare for the move, but finds it difficult to make peace with all that is transpiring. She finds herself saying more than she perhaps should.

EDDA: I stopped by the Christian's Women's League. This gossipy little bureaucrat, ugly as Krampus, told me they can marshal a horse cart at an hour's notice and they'll be happy to take whatever you haven't sold. I told her it wouldn't be enough to fill a whole cart, but apparently it doesn't matter: whether its a footstool or the contents of the Schönbrunn Palace, they send the same dirty cart. I don't see why you don't ship what's left to yourself in Holland. I know he doesn't want to arouse suspicions, but why on earth, after two years, would anyone care?

(Silence. She looks around.)

I was starting to get used to this place. No matter. No point getting attached to things. You're going to have an adventure. Pinchik tells me Rotterdam has one of the tallest buildings in all Europe. I can't imagine why that's necessary, but I suppose it's interesting. And no, I haven't told the Professor anything. I haven't told a human soul he's taking you away. It's a miracle he's back. A miracle. Took his sweet time. After everything he put you through, after he—

(She changes her mind.)

We don't know what goes on. What men do in war. What war does to men. Still, I never took him for a deserter. There's less of him than I remembered. He used to be—what's the word? He'd walk into a room and . . . I remember how you two used to laugh; used to come home at all hours and I'd make you both cups of . . . Now he's sitting in there and tomorrow will be the last day I'll see you in this life of mine and there's something wrong about that, something deeply wrong.

(She crosses her arms, looks away, and is silent.)

How could he live two years without writing you a letter, without any word at all? Eight months in hospital under an assumed name and then a new life in Holland—Yes, I will speak! Men think the minute they leave the room, the world stops turning and we women hang suspended like coats on a hook, waiting to be taken down. It is only they who suffer the indignities of life's progressions. Or is it war? If war can make a man forget his wife, what is the point of it? What do we care for? Nothing!

Information on this playwright may be found at
www.smithandkraus.com.
Click on the WRITERS tab.

Dramatic
Mary Claire, fifteen

After hiding her sister's Greek mythology school project,
the head of Medusa, Mary Claire must persuade Reenie to
go out with her to meet the boys on the beach. Their father
gave Mary Claire permission to go out tonight, but only if
she takes her sister Reenie with her.

MARY CLAIRE: I'm sorry about your "head." It was a joke. I know it's not funny, I'll stop, okay, I swear to God, you can leave it on your dresser or where ever you want, I won't touch it. Okay. It's a good project, it's really good, Reenie, it's just, here's the thing, it's scares me. There's something about it, actually makes me sick to my stomach. The snaky hair with the red tongues they look like they're movin', and those scary eyes, and her mouth all red and stuff, you gotta admit it's pretty gross. But I won't look at it, okay. Put it anywhere you want. Listen. If you come out with us tonight you can do whatever you want. You can be quiet if you want. I won't make fun of you, I promise. What do I have to do to make you say yes? Please, I'm beggin' you, I'm on my knees. And—okay, we're not goin 'to Mary Francese's house. We're really goin' to Rockaway beach. We're gonna sleep on the beach. It's gonna be great: we're gonna build a bonfire, and we'll get high and the guys are coming. Jimmy and Michael and Anthony—I know you like Anthony. I saw him lookin' at you that day you came to get me at the park. It could be your chance with him.

And really this is great if you come that'll be three and three. But—don't worry you don't have to do anything with him if you don't want to. You can sit around the fire while I'm with Jimmy under the boardwalk. You don't have to if you don't want to. Okay? Name it, Reenie, what do I have to do? I'm sorry okay. I'm sorry for everything I ever did, all the mean things I ever said. You're my sister and I just—you just make me mad sometimes the way you stand there and you don't ever say anything; you just follow me around and copy everything I do and say all the time. Or you're not sayin' anything. You should say what you want to say and stop bein' so weird. Errgggg! Like the way you're standin' there right now, you make me say all these things, and you just stand there, I mean, what's wrong with you?

Information on this playwright may be found at
www.smithandkraus.com.
Click on the WRITERS tab.

Dramatic
Brigit, thirty-five

After a violent argument with their father, Bridget tells her two teenaged daughters Reenie and Mary Claire this story as a way of justifying what they just witnessed.

BRIGIT: Last year for the bicentennial I wanted to see the tall ships. I was looking forward to it all year. He knew how much I love Early American. He took me to pick out this furniture. It was on sale because it was almost over. In a week no one was gonna want it no more. We got it cheap. A table, four chairs and a matching hutch. Plus the eagle over the doorway they threw in for free. Says right there: 1776 to 1976. The two hundredth anniversary of this country. That was a big deal to me. It might not have mattered to him, but it mattered to me. And you girls were excited about it too. It was supposed to be the best fireworks ever, shot over the harbor. The only thing I wanted to do was go to the city and see those tall ships comin' in the harbor. I asked him could we go and he said yeah. But when the day came he said he didn't want to drive in all that traffic. All the people, he said. That's why I wanted to go. I wanted to *be* with all the people. He never wants to go to see my family on holidays so they stopped askin' us. We didn't go to my best friend April's weddin', cause he didn't like her husband. He don't like any of my friends, so I lost touch with all of them because of him. But I wanted to go see the tall ships that day. The last minute he didn't *feel* like goin'. So we sat here at this dinin' room table, our elbows stickin' to this fuckin tablecloth. He said be happy you got new furniture.

Information on this playwright may be found at www.smithandkraus.com. *Click on the WRITERS tab.*

Dramatic
Anna, late twenties-early thirties

Anna is a very ambitious Republican political operative, fighting to secure the confirmation of Judge Robert Bork, nominated by President Reagan to the Supreme Court. Her mother-in-law Hester, a socialite and liberal political activist, is fighting to see Bork's nomination rejected by the Senate. Anna finds a draft of a letter Hester has written as part of this campaign, which, when it is printed, might turn the tide against Bork, which will create a huge problem for her son, Colin, who works for a conservative Senator.

ANNA: I'm worried about what this will do to us. *Is* doing. This fight. The prospect of defeat terrifies me because, you see, I think I will be all right, I have guts and I'm ruthless and I'm at Justice, and I will ultimately- find a way to stay in a good place. But Colin—

(Beat.)

Well, Colin works for Senator Gordon Humphrey of New Hampshire, and Gordon Humphrey, should this one go down, may become disgusted and choose not to run again—it's beginning to look that way—and then what is Colin but a man with a resume.

A nice man.

A nice man with a moustache.

(Beat.)

You know what I'm talking about. You marry a man, you marry his bright ambition, his spark, and then you watch, because you can't know, can you, watching a man's life is like watching a movie, a *good* movie, it's not quite predictable. Who will he turn out to be? Will the ambition lead him to something real, something great, or will it flatten out? He likes to cook. It's just—he's looking for ways to live the life lesser men want to live these days. The playground life. The domestic life. Nothing wrong with that except it's not what I'd hoped he'd turn into. Colin needs a victory. His *Senator* needs a victory to keep him in the game, and I am hoping that's enough to bring back Colin's spark. So—tear this up, please. Don't be a part of a defeat that will be very hard for your son.

Seriocomic
Allie, thirties; Tom's wife; Michael's mother;
feisty, irreverent,

During an earlier meeting with Allie and Tom, Claire has
implied that Michael will be terminated from the program,
unless they are willing to choose a genius sperm donor for
their second child too. Tom has been adamant that they
use an 'average' donor this time, so their second child can
be more like him, and Allie had agreed to honor his wish.
However, the meeting ends badly, when Allie changes her
mind, and Tom angrily rushes out. When Claire tells Allie
that she, as the only biological parent, can choose the next
donor without Tom's consent, and that he has no legal
standing to object, Allie is outraged by the mere sugges-
tion that she would exploit her advantage at such a high
cost to Tom. But as she returns to Claire's office an hour
later, she hasn't been able to get the suggestion out of her
mind.

ALLIE: What is it with Gwen? When I bumped into
her at that soup place, she said she was deciding
whether to jump off a bridge. Then she said, "Not
literally," and started begging me to promise not to
tell you, but before I could say "fine," she said, "Oh,
do whatever you want, that's what you always do
anyway" . . . so you know what I think? Fuck her.
(couple of beats, as she tries with diminishing
success to maintain this tone of feisty bravado)
That thing you were saying . . . how I don't need
Tom's signature? He and I were watching this
show about some lesbian couple with a kid, where
the mom who gave birth got custody, and the one

who mostly took care of the kid didn't even get visits. I could tell from Tom's expression he was already comparing our . . . so I said, "Maybe the judge has a prejudice against lesbians" . . . which didn't make any sense since they were both lesbians . . . but then Tom said, "You think she's got it bad, when it comes to family court, you've got worse odds being a man than a lesbian," referring to a guy he knows who came home to find his 12 year son watching porn on TV, with his wife passed out drunk on the couch right next to him, so he grabbed a camera, took pictures to show the judge, and his wife still got the kid, so maybe Tom's right. If someone can lose his kid, because he's only 'the father,' what about guys like Tom who didn't even kick in the sperm?

(slight beat)

That's what you meant, isn't it?

Comic
Phyllida Spotte/Hume, thirties

Phyllida is a female explorer, which is unheard of in Victorian England, and has recently returned from the Lost City of Pahatlabong, bringing back with her a native, whom she calls Luigi. A faction of the heretofore all-male Explorer's Club wants to propose her for membership. She has been invited to the club to make her case as to why she should be made a member.

PHYLLIDA: Gentlemen of the Explorers Club, I thank you. I shall endeavor to prove worthy of the honor you do me. May I present to you all: a genuine warrior of the NaKong tribe of the Lost City of Pahatlabong! Luigi, *na'I haa'ru.* His name is not actually Luigi, but *Loo-ah-JA-mweno-weptanefes-mat- naa'ru-sengway.* Which translates roughly to "Strikes Without Warning And Waters the Ground With Your Blood." I have shortened it to "Luigi" for simplicity's sake. Of my full journey to Pahatlabong, I will say little. It was grueling. Although we had set out well-provided with canned meats, tea, cheap alcohol for the local guides and better quality alcohol for the stove, by the time we reached the island chain of Suk'haaru, we had exhausted everything. Deserted by those guides who had not died of alcohol poisoning, I crawled delirious through the swamps, and when I was found by Luigi, I was in possession of nothing more than the clothes on my back and a spoon . . . Luckily for me, the NaKong god, *Mogweet,* is spoon-shaped. So they greeted me as a messenger from their god. Luigi is a fierce fighter, like all NaKong. They have to be because Pahatlabong is the worst place on earth. The rocky soil cannot be farmed. All the trees have been cut down. They have hunted nearly all the animals to extinction and are forced to subsist on a jerky made of toad. The toad is poisonous. But most of the poison boils off when the toad is poached in urine. But the NaKong will not move from their homeland. They say that long ago their god, Mogweet, commanded them to live there, saying it would make them strong, and when one of them asked why they could not be strong elsewhere, Mogweet grabbed him by the nostrils, flung him to the ground, and jumped up and down on his spine until he was dead. The NaKong celebrate this event every year, like Christmas. Only instead of singing carols and exchanging presents they cower silently in their huts for two days. I will end this lecture here, as tomorrow I will be presenting Luigi to the Queen, and he must rest after his journey, but I would be happy to continue my lecture series on this proud people, if invited back by this esteemed club. Thank you all.

Information on this playwright may be found at
www.smithandkraus.com.
Click on the WRITERS tab.

Comic
Cynthia, twenty-eight

Cynthia is an infamous socialite, Carole Lombard with a heart of darkness, an It Girl, charming, captivating but mean when threatened. In another time she'd be called an alcoholic. In this scene, which takes place in 1937, Cynthia speaks to a mannequin made in her image. She is throwing the mannequin a "debut" party for the press and her society friends.

CYNTHIA: Oh! You gave me a start. Isn't it awful when someone else arrives at a soiree wearing the same dress? My. Well. Aren't you the very picture of grace? Such charm. Imagine it; a mannequin throwing herself a party. Who could have ever come up with it? You know when I was in your shoes making my debut, one couldn't choose to wear a nude colored dress for these sorts of things. No, no. Only white. It's the proper thing, you know. Well, I say fie to proper. I say one should choose one's own color and be one's own person. I did. I did! I'll paint you a picture: there I was at the top of the stair all of sixteen, waiting to be announced. And then it came, my big moment. They said, and now Miss Cynthia Thompson, daughter of Josephine and Winston Thompson. There was a gasp, a few muffled laughs. A whisper. And then. There was nothing. Because I was sliding down the bannister, I, Cynthia Wells, daughter of Lunessa and Charles Wells, landing in the middle of the floor in a tumult. My lip was bloodied. My dress was a stain.

But I didn't look like every other girl in the room anymore, no no no. I didn't look like the next at all . . . I'll be. You. He gave you my scar.

Information on this playwright may be found at
www.smithandkraus.com.
Click on the WRITERS tab.

Comic
Cynthia, twenty-eight

Cynthia is an infamous socialite, Carole Lombard with a heart of darkness, an It Girl, charming, captivating but mean when threatened. In another time she'd be called an alcoholic. In this scene, which takes place in 1937, Cynthia speaks to a mannequin made in her image. She is throwing the mannequin a 'debut' party for the press and her society friends.

CYNTHIA: Oh! You gave me a start. Isn't it awful when someone else arrives at a soiree wearing the same dress? My. Well. Aren't you the very picture of grace? Such charm. Imagine it; a mannequin throwing herself a party. Who could have ever come up with it? You know when I was in your shoes making my debut, one couldn't choose to wear a nude colored dress for these sorts of things. No, no. Only white. It's the proper thing, you know. Well, I say fie to proper. I say one should choose one's own color and be one's own person. I did. I did! I'll paint you a picture: there I was at the top of the stair all of sixteen, waiting to be announced. And then it came, my big moment. They said, and now Miss Cynthia Thompson, daughter of Josephine and Winston Thompson. There was a gasp, a few muffled laughs. A whisper. And then. There was nothing. Because I was sliding down the bannister, I, Cynthia Wells, daughter of Lunessa and Charles Wells, landing in the middle of the floor in a tumult. My lip was bloodied. My dress was a stain. But I didn't look like every other girl in the room anymore, no no no. I didn't look like the next at all . . . I'll be. You. He gave you my scar.

Information on this playwright may be found at
www.smithandkraus.com.
Click on the WRITERS tab.

Dramatic
Natasha, mid-forties

Natasha is a Russian who converted to Judaism to marry Moishe, a kosher butcher and she fanatically follows all the Jewish laws and practices. Natasha and Moishe live with his sister, Bessie, and her husband. Natasha's religious zeal annoys Bessie. Here, Passover is approaching. Natasha is cleaning out the kitchen of all foods forbidden on Passover. She fights with Bessie over a bag of lentils. Natasha says the lentils are forbidden. Bessie says they're not forbidden. Finally, Bessie tells Natasha that she used to be nice before she became a Jew—"What happened to you?"

NATASHA: What happened to me? I'll tell you what happened. Four things happened. Allow me to start with the things you already know. The Bolsheviks killed my father. Is one. This you know. So I came to America. Is two. That you know. One day in America I meet a Jew who tells me it's Moishe Dubrovnik and I can't believe this big man was that little boy I knew from Minsk. Is the third thing, which you know. *(pause)* Fourth thing, you don't know. Why? Because Moishe said, "don't tell Bessie." But now that you have made it a custom to tell me how I used to be nice and am no longer nice, I will tell you the fourth thing once and for always. *(pause)* Moishe and I, we are walking our evening walk by the park, and it's dark from winter and there comes a gang of men, like in Russia who destroyed your home, which I know Moishe remembers with pain in his heart, that he was little boy and could not protect anyone. So these men they call Moishe nasty names, and tell him to go away because the blonde is for them—this is their name for me, "the blonde"— but Moishe does not move. So they come forward, closer to us, and I haven't been so scared since Russia. Then . . . Moishe moves like so.

(She demonstrates a protective movement.)
To defense me by one arm. The other arm? He puts in his coat, and out comes one of his knives

(demonstrating the motion)
not the little one, the great one, for chopping the bones, and he holds like this—

(demonstrating a strong grip)
and the blade is shining in moonlight. And what does he say to those pigs? I'll tell you. He looks straight to them, and he says *(pause)* "So?" And the men, they look like they have seen a ghost, and they run away, and in that moment I said in my heart, not only will I marry this man, I will be to him the best wife he could want. Not pretty good. Not all right. Not satisfactory. The best. *(pause)* If this means I work until I am one-hundred-and-ten-percent Jewish, I am working. If it means, do not daydream on little houses, I am not daydreaming. And if it means no lentils, then no lentils! That is what happened to me.

Information on this playwright may be found at
www.smithandkraus.com.
Click on the WRITERS tab.

Seriocomic
Karen, thirties

Karen is a Major Movie Star. She has invited Steve, the co-star of her next movie and his much younger wife Missy over to dinner at her mansion in the Hollywood Hills to talk over a problematic scene from her next movie. We can barely hear the traffic sounds below, but she finds them them very annoying.

KAREN: OH MY GOD! THAT SOUND! DRIVES ME CRAZY! Can you hear it . . . hear that?!
(Holds up her hand, signaling to MISSY and STEVE,)
God, look at 'em down there!! All those fucking cars on the 101! I hate traffic! That's the one thing about this town—I love my work and the, you know, *fans* and all that, but—the roads are shit!! They really are. You pay so much for a home . . . nice home in the hills and people come to a goddamn stand-still, right in front of our gate . . . right there! It's insane! Police sirens all the time and those . . . like, *emergency* vehicles . . . and you know what? It's gotten to the point where I just started cheering 'em on! No, I do! If I hear a wreck or people sitting on their horns, I'll come out here and I'll just start screaming, YES! YES! YES!! I mean, if I gotta listen to this all the time, then I want blood and fire . . . know what I'm saying? I don't want a goddamn *Suburu* in the diamond lane with a flat tire! No, fuck that! I want bodies and death and, like, *chaos*!! That's what I want!!
(looking back over at STEVE and MISSY)

It's a nice view, though, otherwise. From up here
. . .

> *(She takes a few deep breaths, smiles, collects herself. she moves back toward the others. she bursts into tears.)*

I'm sorry, that's . . . I don't really mean that! I was just—things between Bev and I have been, you know . . . tense! It doesn't matter . . . *(Beat)* God, I'm sorry! Look at me! I'm not usually . . . this is ridiculous!

Dramatic
Car, early forties

Car is attending her 25th high school reunion. She has come upstairs to the choir room, where four of her male classmates are trying to come up with a plan to free Jim, who they think has been kidnapped by terrorists in Chad. She's slightly tipsy. She decides to go back to the party.

CAR: Downstairs is a fucking *death zone.* It's like everyone's looking to be 17 again. But I don't *wanna* be that. I mean—talk about *Jim.* He's *out* there right now—somewhere—*alone.* And the rest of us are here, and we are *not* in high school anymore!— We're *people.* Fully formed people—except for those of us who are divorced and thus *de*-formed, but even *that's* a form of formativeness because it makes us champions, Reg. Just like Jim. And I don't know about *you* guys, but I am an empowered woman of the 21st century—beaten-up but fucking capable of *everything.* Of sticking my hand out and grabbing a handful of life and sticking it in my pocket and walking around and saying to myself, "Yes—there is life here, inside of me, inside my left front pocket and I'm going to *make* something of that life—*with* that life. I'm gonna live like a bull in an igloo and I'm *not* gonna take no for an answer and I'm *NEVER* gonna give into apathy or terror or ignorance or viciousness . . . or a bad fucking marriage. Because we are human beings and that comes with *responsibility. (quieter)* We're post-40 people, and we *may* be divorced and drunk

. . . and . . . and sad. But the *very* least thing we can do is have fun . . . and be prideful and *live fully.*

(silence a moment as they all absorb this . . . and then:)

Anywhoodle. I gotta go. Everyone'll be wondering where you went.

Information on this playwright may be found at
www.smithandkraus.com.
Click on the WRITERS tab.

Dramatic
Stel, fifteen

Stel is living in a house formerly occupied by another family, now exiled. A few weeks before, Joze, the son from that family, made the illegal journey to see his old place, and he and Stel met late at night in the kitchen. Though at first she was frightened of him, eventually she asked him to return. She hasn't told anyone in her family about this meeting, and now she's on the roof of the house, looking out into the distance and wondering if she'll ever see him again.

STEL: In every house, in every town, in every city, in every country—people put on the lights when night comes, but God of Lights, I have nothing to say to you. I asked you to show me, and you showed me, and now I'm sorry I asked. I flipped the light on, and that was my first mistake. I could have just gone on, listening in the dark. Like now. Probably he won't come again. And there's no way for me to find him. At the records office, they said no one lived here before. The only way would be if it all breaks apart—like the centrifuge where you're all thrown against the walls and against the ones next to you, and you can't help touching. *(Pause)* In every house, in every town, in every city, in every country, there are broken things. Broken toys, broken TVs, everyone kicks them and acts like it's such a problem. They don't see the good side. (Pause) Goodbye, God of Light. I call upon you, God of Broken Things. Break the guns, so nothing shoots. Break the tanks, the spyglasses in the watchtowers. The walls, the gates, the prisons, and the locks—all thrown into one, pressed against the earth, spinning. And let him come. Let him come to me then.

Seriocomic
Suzie Q, twelve

Susie Q is the daughter of Dr. and Mrs. Sidney Rosenstein of Ditmas Park, Brooklyn; the year is 1956. She is responding to the audience's question, "What's your secret?"

SUZIE Q: I touched it! I snuck into Robbie's room, and I touched it. The wood is smooth and shiny. And then I touched a string. It was tight. It's a wire. And then I touched another string. And then another and another and another. And then I strummed. It made my thumb feel funny. Robbie would kill me if he knew. Please don't tell my brother. It's our secret, Okay? I'm good at keeping secrets. I think I'm mature for my age. I'm so good at secrets that when I grow up, I want to be a spy. I'll spy on the Russians. They're the bad guys. My brother wants to be a rocker when he grows up. Rockers are bad seeds. I heard my parents talking. I'm very mature for my age. I think I know what a bad seed is. Don't tell anyone, but . . . I love bad seeds. When I'm sixteen, I'll have my Sweet Sixteen and then I'll get to go to all the parties. Parties where they rock and roll. My dream is to meet Elvis Presley. He's a real bad seed. 'Cuz of the guitar. I saw Elvis Presley on the TV. We have one. We always watch the Ed Sullivan Show on Sunday nights. Sometimes I can't get to sleep thinking of Elvis. He's simply dreamy. I draw pictures of my dreams. I'm always dreaming about the moon. My teacher says whoever gets to the moon first will rule the world. I think the moon belongs to everybody. It's a special place. If I got to spy on the Russians, that's where I'd go: To the moon. I would see everything from there. Oh no! I have to go. The Good Humor truck is coming down the street!

Dramatic
Bree Benson, forty-four

Bree is an official with the National Security Agency, here talking to a State Dept. official who has told her that the guy they sent over to the Vatican to try and persuade the Pope not to go to Damascus just before the U.S. bombs it because they think the Syrians mastermined a terrorist bombing in New York has, for reasons State does not know, resigned.

BREE: He has resigned? Is that what you're telling me, Bowles? This fuck has resigned? You're standing there telling me he has *resigned*? Is it possible to fuck up an assignment more than you people have fucked this up! It is unbelievable. You're not to blame? Well then WHO is to blame? The Angel Moroni? You're not to blame? I don't give a shit what you are saying, or what you think you are saying or what you think you think you want to say, Bowles. I only want to hear one thing out of you. What the fuck are you doing about it? Why are you continuing to stand here with your mouth open and your brain shut while this loose cannon is wandering around Europe vomiting up Jesus Christ only knows what state secrets to any subversive organization who dangles some piece of ass in front of him. Somebody can grab him and take him hostage! How would that make us look if some trumped up fucking liberation front acting in the name of who knows what insane pack of religious fanatics ends up decapitating him on prime television for the whole fucking world to see! How would that make us look? That ever occur to you, Bowles? That ever occur to anyone over there in State? Find this fuck! Stop talking and get the hell out of here and find him! Find him and bring him in.

Dramatic
Nadia Kirilenko, late thirties to early forties

Nadia, a Chenchen Muslim, is a reported for PanArabya television. She has gone to the Vatican to meet with the Pope, an old friend and the first African pontiff, who plans to fly to Damascus while he thinks will prevent the American from bombing it into rubble in retaliation for a terrorist bombing in New York which the U.S. government thinks was master-minded by the Syrians. She wants an exclusive, but she also doesn't want him to go.

NADIA: Okay. I will give this to you as straight as I can, because I can't imagine anything less would be of any use to you. I don't believe in what you're doing. I'm not an idealist, and I never thought you were either. I don't believe in anything. I had to fight religion since I was a child to get what I wanted. And then when I became a journalist, all I covered were wars and atrocities perpetrated on each other by people of faith, by idealists and fanatics, by God-worshippers, and Jesus lovers, and Jews, and people who thought they should kill you for eating pork, and other people who thought they were divinely ordained to kill you because you ate beef. I was part of a television crew that filmed an American evangelical aid worker being beheaded, and after the beheading I interviewed the murderer. I hate religion. I hate all religions. I hate people of faith. I hate faith because it thwarts human life. You go to Damascus, you will probably be killed. The Americans don't care, that gang in Damascus doesn't care. All the good work you've done in

Africa did not come from your being a Catholic, from being anything, from having faith. You did good work, and risked your life, because you are a good man. And now you're going to kill yourself for some stupid and indefensible notion that faith in anything can eventually prevail. It can't prevail. The fanatics prevail. They always prevail. But you don't have to lend them a helping hand.

They don't need a helping hand.

Dramatic
Aimee, twenties

In that awkward moment after a one-night stand, where the question is, should I stay or should I go, Aimee is politely told she should go.

AIMEE : You know what really makes me mad besides the fact that I hate myself for once again putting myself in this position is that I was all determined to wake up this morning, share a good, buttery piece of wheat toast and a strong cup of coffee, look you in the eyes, cutting through all the embarrassment which, until now, I thought wouldn't really be there because so far this was the best just-happened-to-meet-and-really-really-hit-it-off kind of night, and tell you I completely understand that this just is what it is. That I don't have any expectations. I don't want us to get married. I don't want us to have babies. I'm not moving to Portland and you're not going to move to New York. And that I had a lovely time. A really, really lovely twenty-four hours. And I'm not even the kind of person who uses the word lovely. But that's what this is. Or was. And I was going to wish you the best, and tell you that even if your stupid dissertation committee thinks you're a fool, I don't, and that you should go back to Portland knowing that one person did hear you, and that one person did believe you, and that should be enough. And most important, I wanted you to know that this was not a revenge screw, but a wonderful night with the best, nicest, weepiest guy I've ever met. And I loved every minute. *(beat)* But that's what I was going to say.

Dramatic
Audrey, Sixties

*Here Audrey, an actress, tells her daughter Kitty the true
story of why she left Kitty's father when Kitty was a baby.*

AUDREY: I loved your father. Very much. I did. You
think I kept you from him because I hated him.
That's not true. I loved him. I can still see him. He
was so handsome. Movie star handsome. Thick,
black hair and eyes, blue eyes. And charm. My
god, he made me laugh. But he was also, I don't
know . . . so unhappy. He drank, a lot. I never did.
He couldn't stop. He drank and when he drank he
hit me. And he was sorry. He'd be sorry, And he'd
cry. And then the sun came out and we were happy. He was a machinist, worked on cars. He loved
them. I never thought I'd love a man like that. But
I did. Dirty hands. Blue eyes. My mother thought
I could do better. Well, I did better, eventually. In
some ways. I thought I could figure him out, you
know, what the problem was. I couldn't. Months
would pass with everything perfect, and then out of
the blue . . . But when you were born I thought, this
is it, what he needs, what we need. And it was eight
months or nine, he didn't drink. A happy time. You
were one when we decided, he and I together, that
it was time. That you should have a brother. We
didn't have much money, but we didn't care. And I
got pregnant. And I was happy. And he was happy.
You were one, so you were happy. We *decided* it
was a boy. I named him Jason. Your brother inside

of me. I was four months pregnant when it happened. We went to the park, the three of us, well, four. I bought some peanuts from a man with a cart and he told me I was pretty. And there were no clouds and the sun was hot. When we got home, I put you in the crib and he didn't talk, your father. And I knew something was wrong. He went out. And I fed you. And it started to rain. And when he got home, when your father got home, he was very wet and very drunk. And furious. Raging, like an animal. Furious. He decided, in his head that I was flirting—with the man, from the park, which wasn't true. He was screaming, you were screaming. And he hit me. On my face, on my neck. You were crying. I fought back. He pushed me down. I got up and he pushed me again. And he threw a lamp and glass fell into your crib. And he kicked me. You were screaming, I was crying and he kicked me, and he died, Jason died. Your father killed him. I *knew* him. And your father killed him. For a long time you had a small scar on your arm from the glass in the crib. You were a baby, my baby. I *had* to leave. He'd kill you or me or both of us . . . He begged and he threatened. But there were scars. Bruises, black eyes and scars on my legs. So I made him a deal. I offered a deal. I promised him I would never tell anyone, I'd never say it, what happened to me, or to you, or to Jason. Not the police, or his father, or you or anyone ever. I promised him. And all he had to do, was never see you again.

Information on this playwright may be found at
www.smithandkraus.com.
Click on the WRITERS tab.

Comic
Chloe, twenties to thirties

Chloe has a theory that literary characters actually exist,
which she shares with two friends.

CHLOE: So, William Shakespeare wrote *Hamlet.*
Okay? He creates this character. *(as Shakespeare)*
"Here's me writing about this tight-assed Dane
whose life is going down the crapper." And so,
poof! Somewhere out there, Hamlet comes into existence. Like, a real person. I'm not talking about
fucking historical fucking Hamlet. I'm talking
about fucking William fucking Shakespeare's fucking Hamlet. When you create a work of fiction,
you literally create that world. It's out there.
Somewhere. You are that world's god. And you
don't even know it! Somewhere there's a world
where *Hamlet* really happened, and Shakespeare
is god of that world. There's another world where
Pride and Prejudice is true, and Jane Austen is
goddess there. And somewhere, in some pathetic
shithole, there's a world where *Twilight* is real,
and the god of that world is whoever the fuck
that person is who wrote *Twilight.* It's a working theory. Just bear with me. So, get this. Imagine you're Hamlet. You're Hamlet, and your life
is suckville. You're like, what is this? *(as Hamlet)*
"My uncle kills my dad, my mom's a total whore,
my girlfriend's this suicidal hippy-dippy bitch, and
pretty much everyone I know is getting stabbed
or poisoned. What's up with that?" You got a life

like that, you'd pray to God, and say, "Hey, God, why does my life have to be this frickin' vale of tears? What's up with that shit?" This world has a god. Shakespeare. So, imagine this scenario. Hamlet meets God, who's Shakespeare, and he's like, what the fuck, dude? Why'd you make my life such a mess? And what would Shakespeare say? What *could* he say? "Sorry, guy, I had to make your life be a shitstorm so that people could enjoy a good tragedy. No hard feelings." I mean, can you imagine that? Your life is a fucking carbonated cesspool just so a bunch of other people can be entertained. And it's not just Hamlet, not just Shakespeare. Look at, what, Peter Rabbit. Peter Fucking Rabbit! His creator-goddess is Beatrix Potter and she sends that psychopathic bastard Mr. MacGregor after him. Why? Just to give the kids a laugh. Is that crazy, or what?

Information on this playwright may be found at
www.smithandkraus.com.
Click on the WRITERS tab.

VEILS

Tom Coash

Dramatic
Intisar, Eighteen to Twenty-five

Intisar is an African-American Muslim, 18-25 years old and wears a veil (hijab) that is wrapped snugly around her head, covering her hair but not her face. "Inti" is a strong-willed, intelligent, passionate young woman who is doing a year abroad at the American Egyptian University in Cairo. She is delivering this monologue to a video camera to post on her Egyptian roommate Samar's internet blog. Together they are making blog videos addressing women's issues and, in particularly, the controversial custom of veiling. So, in essence, she is addressing the world.

INTISAR: I want to answer a few questions about this, my veil, my hijab. No, it is not hot. No, my father doesn't make me wear it. No, I don't wear it in the shower. And no, I am not oppressed. 9/11, 2001, right? My mother was forced to strip to her underwear in the back room of an airport. I was thirteen and we were flying home from my aunt's wedding. Halfway there our plane was diverted to a small airport. Nobody knew what was happening. We didn't know of the hijackings or that all flights were being grounded. We were on the runway for more than an hour when airport security came on the plane. Searching, apparently, for anybody who looked dangerous and proceeded to escort my Mother and me onto the tarmac, everybody staring. In a back room full of security, they had our suitcases open, belongings strewn all over, and my mother was requested to submit to a body search. When she refused, the requests became uglier, strip or be arrested. She looked at me, afraid, tears running down my face, and she took her clothes off. Of course they found nothing. What was there to find? They looked at me and she said "You will NOT undress my daughter." They didn't but they made me take my veil off. Why is that? It was my first veil. When a girl reaches puberty. Delicate, light blue. Like the sky we had been flying through. A proud moment. Becoming a woman. A rite of passage. I hadn't had it a month and a person of supposed authority forced me take it off. Raghead. Later I sat crying next to my mother as we waited for my father to drive 400 miles to rescue us. She said "Why are you crying?" "Shame." "Daughter . . . another person cannot inflict shame on you. Only you can inflict shame on yourself. When those men looked at my body, my naked skin, they were the ones who felt shame. Because God was not in their hearts. Keep God strong in your heart and you will never feel shame." They kept asking my mother where we were from. Like we weren't American. Like we were foreigners. She would say "Overbrook Park." "Where is that?" "Philadelphia." And they would look at her like she was making a joke. What was she supposed to say? Africa? Fula? 70 Futa Toro? Where my great, great, great grandmother was stolen out of her bed, raped, and dragged to America in chains? And the first thing they did, when she got to the Land of the Free, was strip her naked and put her on the auction block . . . she wasn't hiding anything either. The right to wear clothes, to cover yourself, is important to my family. This veil connects me to my God, to my family, and to our history of struggle. When I put on this veil, I know who I am. There is a simplicity. A clarity. I know who I am and who I want to be. This veil is not hiding away. For me it is a release. Without it I feel naked. I am naked. "Tell the believing women to lower their gaze and be modest, and to display of their adornment only that which is apparent, and to draw their veils over their bosoms." That seems pretty clear to me. God says wear a veil, you do it, right? I believe in this. I am strong in my heart and I'm not hiding anything.

Information on this playwright may be found at
www.smithandkraus.com.
Click on the WRITERS tab.

Dramatic
Vonnie Wolf, fifteen

*In the autumn of 1897, in Armitage, a town in east Ohio,
Vonnie Wolf, age 15, is cast as Juliet in a local produc-
tion of Romeo and Juliet. Pitt Rooks, 14, a poor kid whose
family runs the junkyard by the town dump, cast as a comic servant, is in love with her, and has earlier in the day
revealed to her that he's seen her in a very compromis-
ing position with the director of the play, her high school
teacher. He has threatened to expose the affair, or to kill
the director. In this scene, after rehearsal, Vonnie is sitting
on the back porch at her father's store late at night, and
Pitt has appeared. He hasn't told or killed the director,
but he wants to know why she would let the older man
touch her. Vonnie is very beautiful, very smart, and a gifted
actress. But she is very unhappy at home, and her father
seems cold and distant to her. Here she tries to answer
Pitt's question.*

VONNIE: I've been thinking about it. About what you
asked me. Why I would let him touch me. I'm still
not sure I know the answer. It wasn't anything I
thought about before it happened. And I don't think
he planned on it happening. I really don't. He was
just talking to me about the scene. And he looked at
me. And his eyes were so sad. And then he kissed
me. I think part of the reason I liked it was because
he seemed so sad. I felt bad for him. Because he
was so sad. And then, I just, I don't know. He was
holding me. And it felt so good to be needed. My
father never holds me. Nobody's ever held me like
that. He just seemed to need me so much. *(Pause)*
He loves his wife. It's not because he doesn't love

his wife. I think maybe it's the play. I mean, not just the play. He's unhappy. But not because he doesn't love his wife. It's like the play speaks to him in some way that he can't explain to her. But I understand. I don't mean in any rational way. I mean when I play her. Because most of the time I don't feel like anybody. But when I play her, I'm somebody. I'm her. Even though she doesn't exist. She only existed in the mind of some long dead Englishman. Who was also, I think, very sad. But somehow, when I play her, when I say the words, I turn into somebody in his mind. Somebody he's been longing for. And it's in the girl in the play. And when I become her, I become that, and he needs that. That's what he loves. Not me. He might think he's in love with me. But he's in love with something else. Somebody he can never touch. Does that make any sense to you?

Seriocomic
Viva, twenty-nine

Viva is speaking to her sister-in-law Bridget and her new husband Eddie. Eddie left immediately after their wedding to be with his sister at their grandmother's deathbed without saying good-bye. Viva has just arrived unexpectedly at the house in New Jersey after flying in from California to find him. Jason, Eddie's best friend and a member of the wedding party, fainted in the middle of their wedding ceremony two day before.

VIVA: You must be Bridget! I'm so happy to finally meet you after all those adorable emails! I was going crazy planning the wedding and it was such a relief to know that someone out there had a sense of humor about the whole thing. And can I say, the weather is gorgeous, it's a day to make California jealous. Eddie always talks about the humidity and the green flies, but today is just perfect. I mean the weather, of course, I am so, so sorry about your gramma, Bridget, you must just be shattered to pieces. I've got another big bag in the trunk, I over-packed, I just couldn't think of what to bring and all our things were everywhere. Eddie bear, we still had to pay for the last night in the hotel so I let Jason stay there after talking him down for hours. Sweetheart, he was so upset about fainting like that. But I just let him know that's just how life works, it doesn't have any cosmic significance, and we were just happy he didn't get hurt! I must look a mess, I really apologize for looking like such a wreck . . . What a cute little house! Eddie bear, you haven't even shaved, were you too tired to put on pajamas? Oh, Bridget, we must be making a terrible impression on you! I've just got this other big bag out there in the car . . . That man is such a dear. Really, Bridget, I love your brother, I married the best man on earth. Now what can we do? How can we help? And certainly don't worry about a thing, we missed you in the wedding party but we figured out a new configuration. Jason offered to be the odd usher out and that's how he ended up next to that lamp, I felt so terrible, it was all my fault but I was just so distracted! Did you decide to have the funeral meal in a restaurant? I think that's the best move, really, especially after she suffered so much in this house. You don't want people coming over after that! Eddie and I are family, of course, so it doesn't matter for us. What can I do for you? These are such sad circumstances to meet under! I really thought we were going to lay eyes on each other for the first time at my wedding. And what's this? Old pictures! You have got to be the most organized girl on earth. I would be just clawing my eyes out and you've made time for the important things.

Seriocomic
Nicole, teens to twenties

Nicole describes her idea of Heaven to her boyfriend.

NICOLE: I think heaven always has green grass and hot water in the shower. They'll be lots of blues and golds and you won't care where the other people went to college or what sort of music they like. Every sunset will be worth sitting down and watching until the last sliver slides beneath the horizon, with a million shades of purple and pink plastering the sky. There will always be enough shooting stars in the blue-black night for everyone to make a wish. The capital is a spectacular city with the best-designed buildings, very efficient and sleek but inviting and they make you proud to call it home. No exhaust, no chipped teeth, no despair, no hangovers. Every morning you wake up feeling like you slept the perfect amount of sleep. Deep, interesting, powerful conversations between good friends will go on for hours, days, decades. All the mysteries of the universe will be explained to you and you'll say, 'oh, duh, of course that's it. It's obvious.' Every day you could go sledding or collect seashells on a warm beach or just listen to songbirds while snoozing in a hammock a million times more comfortable than anything on Earth. You can attempt French cuisine and it will come out perfect on your first try. The hot chocolate will be unbelievable. No one cares if you stay up late or sleep in late or wake up at six in the morning and do yoga. Coffee breath won't exist. Feeling stupid won't exist. Hangnails won't exist. Sales tax won't exist. Alzheimer's won't exist. It's always happy hour and the other people at the bar always have funny things to say. No one is ever, ever passive aggressive. It's totally cool to dance in public, even when there is no music. You will whistle melodies that cause people to weep and laugh at the same time. There will be colors we don't even have words for. Unbridled joy. Unbridled joy will be how you describe what you feel all the time in heaven. It's like that moment when you were a kid and got in a big fight with your mom and then, hours later, realized how much you loved her and ran up and gave her a big hug and you both cried. But that feeling is intensified exponentially and lasts for eternity. The feeling will be like ten thousand first kisses.

Dramatic
Roz, fifties

Roz is an inner city school teacher. Here she speaks to Molly, a young teacher at an upscale private high school, about a student she's been tutoring.

ROZ: Tenth grade, can't read. Seriously. This poor kid—he should not be in this section. He needs a reading specialist. So I meet with him after school and try to—I don't know—do something for him. I keep copies of job applications—not Microsoft or anything. Realistic—fast food places. Wal-Mart. And we work on—I mean, if he can at least fill one out maybe he can . . . I don't know. He can't read, Molly. I can be idealistic or realistic—can't do both. So, I try and get him into a program where he can get help. But I need the mother's permission so I go to the house last September to get her to sign the papers. What a piece of work. TV's on the whole time I'm there so I'm competing with Maury Povich. Anyway, she won't sign the papers. Won't let him go. Starts screaming, "My baby's not stupid." I just want to grab this woman by the throat and scream back, "He is stupid! But maybe I can make him a little less stupid." Jesus . . . you need a license to drive. You have to register to vote. But they let anybody reproduce. And this poor kid— you know—he's so frustrated . . . you can see it . . . I can see it in his eyes, he just . . . what's gonna' happen to him? Kid doesn't stand a chance. He's doomed. I don't know what to do . . .

(forcing a smile)
And he's huge too. Feel like I'm doing *Of Mice and Men*.

Dramatic
Shatique, twenties, African-American

Shatique is speaking with Ray, a middle aged white man with whom she rides a bus every Saturday. The bus goes to a prison, and here she gives Ray a quick lesson on protocol she goes through to visit her brother. She also has the habit of trying to correct her improper grammar.

SHATIQUE: They treat us like dirt. Give 'em a uniform and minimum wage and they all—
> *(correcting herself)*

They're all—look at me. I'm Mr. Authority Figure. I'm a fat, stupid loser at home so I'll push you folks around. I mean, I expect it from the white ones but even the—
> *(She catches herself)*

S'posed to be two hours but it never is. Start the clock the minute you go into they—their—waitin' area. "Line up against the wall, arms at your side, any purses or packages on the floor in front of your feet." Got it memorized, I could work there. Then they go get him and you just gotta' sit there. Half hour sometimes. Can't even take a magazine in with ya. Ya sit there. They don't care. Most of the whole visit's just waitin'. Wait ta get in. Wait to get searched. Line for the metal detector. And always some—
> *(Catches herself before "asshole")*

Ya know, somebody got to hold it up for somethin' stupid.

(Lowers her voice and points.)

First timer. She not even gonna' get in. Way she's dressed. That skirt. Not even close to coverin' her ass.

(by rote)

"Visitors should use good taste and discretion in dress at all times. Short skirts, halter tops or clothing made of see-through material are strictly forbidden." Now I got a dollar says she throws a fit when they tell her no and she holds up the whole line. She shouldn't wear that skirt in public anyway. Not with that ass. And that one? Piercings everywhere. I mean *every-where*. Don't get behind her at the metal detector. That's why I always sit at the front here. Get in before the rest of 'em. *(silence)* Degrading . . . seriously so . . . like we're the criminals.

(forcing a quiet laugh)

'Course some'a these women—who knows? *(silence)* The dogs are the worst part. Ya know, sniffin' for drugs and stuff. Walk up and down the line there. Back and forth. Look like somethin' outta' the Nazis. And every week I get—hands get all sweaty and my heart starts beatin' like crazy. Every damn week I get scared they're gonna' find somethin' and I know for a fact they got nothin' to find. Not on me they don't.

(Silence; she darkens a moment.)

One time I saw a girl I knew from high school on here. Goin' to see her boyfriend. She was with her mom—who was goin' to see *her* boyfriend.

(more to herself)

No woman ever comin' out here to see my boy. I don't care what I gotta' do.

These monologues may be used for auditions, classes, contests, competitions, readings and workshops, without payment of royalty.

AMERICAN HERO © 2014 by Bess Wohl. Reprinted by permission of Chris Till, Creative Artists Agency. Published by Dramatists Play Service. For performance rights, contact Dramatists Play Service, 440 Park Ave. S., New York, NY 10016 (www.dramatists.com) (212-683-8960).

AMERICAN MIDGET © 2014 by Jonathan Yukich. Reprinted by permission of Jonathan Yukich. Published by Broadway Play Publishing. For performance rights, Broadway Play Publishing, (212-772-8334), (www.broadwayplaypubl.com).

ANNAPURNA © 2011 by Sharr White. Reprinted by permission of Amy Hasselbeck, William Morris Endeavor. Published by Dramatists Play Service. For performance rights, contact Dramatists Play Service, 440 Park Ave. S., New York, NY 10016 (www.dramatists.com) (212-683-8960).

APPROPRIATE © 2012 by Brandon Jacobs-Jenkins. Reprinted by permission of Amy Hasselbeck, William Morris Endeavor. Published by Dramatists Play Service. For performance rights, contact Dramatists Play Service, 440 Park Ave. S., New York, NY 10016 (www.dramatists.com) (212-683-8960).

BAUER © 2014 by Lauren Gunderson. Reprinted by permission of Kate Navin, The Gersh Agency. For performance rights, contact Kate Navin (knavin@gershny.com).

BIG BOSSMAN © 2014 by Peter Ullian. Reprinted by permission of Susan Gurman, Susan Gurman Agency. Published by Broadway Play Publishing.For performance rights, contact Broadway Play Publishing, (212-772-8334), (www.broadwayplaypubl.com).

BLOOD MOON © 2013 by Lila Feinberg. Reprinted by permission of Jared Weber, ICM Partners. For performance rights, contact Di Glazer, ICM Partners (dglazer@icmpartners.com).

BUG STUDY © 2014 by Emma Goldman-Sherman. Reprinted by permission of Emma Goldman-Sherman. For performance rights, contact Emma Goldman-Sherman (emmagoldmansherman@gmail.com).

BY THE WATER © 2014 by Sharyn Rothstein. Reprinted by permission of Jared Weber, ICM Partners. Published by Dramatists Play Service. For performance rights, contact Dramatists Play Service, 440 Park Ave. S., New York, NY 10016 (www.dramatists.com) (212-683-8960).

CAFÉ © 2012 by Raquel Almazan. Reprinted by permission of Raquel Almazan. For performance rights, contact Raquel Almazon (raquelalmazon@hotmail.com).

CAUGHT © 2014 by Christopher Chen. Reprinted by permission of Antje Oegel, AO International. For performance rights, contact Antje Oegel (aoegel@aoiagency.com).

CHALK FARM © 2013 by Kieran Hurley & AJ Taudevin. Reprinted by permission of Andrew Walby, Oberon Books Ltd. Published by Oberon Books Ltd. For performance rights, contact Susan Blakely, The Agency (sblakely@theagency.co.uk).

CHILD SOLDIER © 2014 by J. Thalia Cunningham. Reprinted by permission of J. Thalia Cunningham. For performance rights, contact J. Thalia Cunningham (thalia@nycap.rr.com).

CONSTANT STATE OF PANIC © 2008 by Patrick Gabridge. Reprinted by permission of Patrick Gabridge. For performance rights, contact Patrick Gabridge (pat@gabridge.com).

CREATING CLAIRE © 2014 by Joe DiPietro. Reprinted by permission of Scott Yoselow, The Gersh Agency. Published by Dramatists Play Service. For performance rights, contact Dramatists Play Service, 440 Park Ave. S., New York, NY 10016 (www.dramatists.com) (212-683-8960).

DAFFODILS © 2014 by Daniel Guyton. Reprinted by permission of Daniel Guyton. For performance rights, contact Daniel Guyton (dguyton21@gmail.com).

DEAD AND BREATHING © 2014 by Chisa Hutchinson. Reprinted by permission of Mary Harden, Harden-Curtis Assoc. For performance rights, contact Mary Harden (maryharden@hardencurtis.com).

DEAD SPECIAL CRABS © 2014 by Dan Kitrosser. Reprinted by permission of Dan Kitrosser. For performance rights, contact Jonathan Mills, Paradigm Agency (jmills@paradigmagency.com).

DETAINEE © 2014 by Sam Graber. Reprinted by permission of Sam Graber. For performance rights, contact Sam Graber (samgraber@comcast.net).

DETROIT '67 © 2012 by Dominique Morisseau. Reprinted by permission of Jonathan Mills, Paradigm Agency. Published by Samuel French, Inc. For performance rights, contact Samuel French, Inc., (212-206-8990), (www.samuelfrench.com).

EVERYTHING THAT'S BEAUTIFUL © 2015 by Elyzabeth Gregory Wilder. Reprinted by permission of Beth Blickers, Abrams Artists. For performance rights, contact Beth Blickers (beth.blickers@abramsartny.com).

EVERYTHING YOU TOUCH © 2015 by Sheila Callaghan. Reprinted by permission of Chris Till, Creative Artists Agency. For performance rights, contact Chris Till (ctill@caa.com).

THE EXCEPTIONALS © 2014 by Bob Clyman. Reprinted by permission of Alexis Williams, Bret Adams Ltd. Published by Broadway Play Publishing. For performance rights, contact Broadway Play Publishing, (212-772-8334), (www.broadwayplaypubl.com).

THE EXPLORER'S CLUB © 2013 by Nell Benjamin. Reprinted by permission of Amy Hasselbeck, William Morris Endeavor. Published by Dramatists Play Service. For performance rights, contact Dramatists Play Service, 440 Park Ave. S., New York, NY 10016 (www.dramatists.com) (212-683-8960).

FILM CHINOIS © 2008 by Damon Chua. Reprinted by permission of Damon Chua. For performance rights, contact Damon Chua (nomadzenn@gmail.com).

THE GABA GIRL © 2015 by Cheri Magid. Reprinted by permission of Beth Blickers, Abrams Artists. For performance rights, contact Beth Blickers (beth.blickers@abramsartny.com).

GHOSTS IN THE COTTONWOODS © 2010 by Adam Rapp. Reprinted by permission of Rachel Viola, United Talent Agency. Published by Broadway Play Publishing. For performance rights, contact Broadway Play Publishing, (212-772-8334), (www.broadwayplaypubl.com).

HATE MAIL © 2013 by Daniel Guyton. Reprinted by permission of Daniel Guyton. For performance rights, contact Daniel Guyton (dguyton21@gmail.com).

HIGH POWERED © 2014 by Dominique Morisseau. Reprinted by permission of Jonathan Mills, Paradigm Agency. For performance rights, contact Jonathan Mills (jmills@paradigmagency.com).

HOLY LAND © 2014 by Mohamed Kacimi, transl. by Chantal Bilodeau. Reprinted by permission of Beth Blickers, Abrams Artists. For performance rights, contact Beth Blickers (beth.blickers@abramsartny.com).

IMPENETRABLE © 2014 by Mia McCullough. Reprinted by permission of Mia McCullough. For performance rights, contact Mia McCullough (brazenhussy@miamccullough.net).

THE INVENTION OF THE LIVING ROOM © 2011 by Andrew R. Heinze. Reprinted by permission of Andrew R. Heinze. For performance rights, contact Andrew R. Heinze (arheinze@gmail.com).

KILL ME, PLEASE! © 2011 by Rhea MacCallum. Reprinted by permission of Rhea MacCallum. Published by Smith & Kraus, Inc. in *2015 The Best 10-Minute Plays*. For performance rights, contact Rhea MacCallum (rheamac@yahoo.com).

LAMP POST © 2013 by Don Nigro. Reprinted by permission of Don Nigro. For performance rights, contact Samuel French, Inc., (212-206-8990), (www.samuelfrench.com.)

LASSO OF TRUTH © 2014 by Carson Kreitzer. Reprinted by permission of Bruce Ostler, Bret Adams Ltd. For performance rights, contact Bruce Ostler (bostler@bretadamsltd.net).

LINES IN THE DUST © 2014 by Nikkole Salter. Reprinted by permission of Nikkole Salter. For performance rights, contact Alexis Williams, Bret Adams Ltd. (awilliams@bretadamsltd.net).

LITTLE CHILDREN DREAM OF GOD © 2014 by Jeff Augustin. Reprinted by permission of Mark Orsini, Bret Adams Ltd. For performance rights, contact Mark Orsini (morsini@bretadamsltd.net).

LOCKDOWN WITH PINKY © 2014 by C.S. Hanson. Reprinted by permission of C.S. Hanson. Published by Applause Theatre & Cinema Books in *25 10-Minute Plays for Teens*. For performance rights, contact C.S. Hanson (cshansonplays@yahoo.com).

MALA HIERBA © 2014 by Tanya Saracho. Reprinted by permission of Mark Orsini, Bret Adams Ltd. Published by Applause Theatre & Cinema Books in *The Best Plays of 2014*. For performance rights, contact Mark Orsini (morsini@bretadamsltd.net).

MINE © 2015 by Laura Marks. Reprinted by permission of Jessica Amato, The Gersh Agency. Published by Dramatists Play Service. For performance rights, contact Dramatists Play Service, 440 Park Ave. S., New York, NY 10016 (www.dramatists. com) (212-683-8960).

MISS MARX or THE INVOLUNTARY SIDE EFFECTS OF LIVING © 2015 by Philip Dawkins. Reprinted by permission of Carrie Granatelli, Dramatic Publishing Co. Published by Dramatic Publishing Co. For performance rights, contact Dramatic Publishing Co. (www.dramaticpublishing.com)

THE MONEY SHOT © 2014 by Neil LaBute. Reprinted by permission of Tracy Carns, Overlook Press. Published by Overlook Press and Dramatists Play Service. For performance rights, contact Dramatists Play Service, 440 Park Ave. S., New York, NY 10016 (www.dramatists.com) (212-683-8960).

MOTHERS AND SONS © 2014 by Terrence McNally. Reprinted by permission of Amy Hasselbeck, William Morris Endeavor. Published by Dramatists Play Service. For performance rights, contact Dramatists Play Service, 440 Park Ave. S., New York, NY 10016 (www.dramatists.com) (212-683-8960).

THE MUSCLES IN OUR TOES © 2014 by Stephen Belber. Reprinted by permission of Jared Weber, ICM Partners. Published by Dramatists Play Service. For performance rights, contact Dramatists Play Service, 440 Park Ave. S., New York, NY 10016 (www.dramatists.com) (212-683-8960).

NDEBELE FUNERAL © 2010 by Zoey Martinson. Reprinted by permission of Zoey Martinson. For performance rights, contact Zoey Martinson (smokemirrors.co@gmail.com).

NIGHTS AT THE STRAY DOG CAFÉ © 2014 by Don Nigro. Reprinted by permission of Don Nigro. For performance rights, contact Samuel French, Inc., (212-206-8990), (www.samuelfrench.com).

NOVEL © 2015 by Anna Ziegler. Reprinted by permission of Anna Ziegler. For performance rights, contact Seth Glewen, The Gersh Agency (sglewen@gershny.com)

OUT OF WATER © 2008 by Brooke Berman. Reprinted by permission of Brooke Berman. For performance rights, contact Brooke Berman (brookeberman@gmail.com).

THE OWL GIRL © 2014 by Monica Raymond. Reprinted by permission of Monica Raymond. For performance rights, contact Monica Raymond (femmevox@hotmail.com).

PA'S HAT © 2005 by Cori Thomas. Reprinted by permission of Ron Gwiazda, Abrams Artists. For performance rights, contact Ron Gwiazda (ron.gwiazda@abramsartny.com).

PENDRAGON COUNTY GHOSTS © 2004 by Don Nigro. Reprinted by permission of Don Nigro. For performance rights, contact Samuel French, Inc., (212-206-8990), (www.samuelfrench.com).

THE PHOTO ALBUM © 2014 by C.S. Hanson. Reprinted by permission of C.S. Hanson. For performance rights, contact C.S. Hanson (cshansonplays@yahoo.com).

POZ (+) © 2014 by Michael Aman. Reprinted by permission of Barbara Hogenson. For performance rights, contact Barbara Hogenson (bhogenson@aol.com).

A QUESTION OF WORDS © 2012 by Richard Manley. Reprinted by permission of Richard Manley. For performance rights, contact Richard Manley (antiqueroman@yahoo.com).

RASHEEDA SPEAKING © 2015 by Joel Drake Johnson. Reprinted by permission of Mark Orsini, Bret Adams Ltd. For performance rights, contact Mark Orsini (morsini@bretadamsltd.net).

REPAIRING A NATION © 2015 by Nikkole Salter. Reprinted by permission of Alexis Williams, Bret Adams Ltd. For performance rights, contact Alexis Williams (awilliams@bretadamsltd.net).

THE ROAD TO DAMASCUS © 2007 by Tom Dulack. Reprinted by permission of Penny Luedtke, The Luedtke Agency. For performance rights, contact Penny Luedtke (pennyagent@gmail.com).

THE RORSCHACH PLAY © 2015 by Kelly Younger. Reprinted by permission of Kelly Younger. For performance rights, contact Kelly Younger (kellyyounger@me.com).

THE RORSCHACH PLAY © 2015 by Kelly Younger. Reprinted by permission of Kelly Younger. For performance rights, contact Kelly Younger (kellyyounger@me.com).

THE RORSCHACH PLAY © 2015 by Kelly Younger. Reprinted by permission of Kelly Younger. For performance rights, contact Kelly Younger (kellyyounger@me.com).

THE RORSCHACH PLAY © 2015 by Kelly Younger. Reprinted by permission of Kelly Younger. For performance rights, contact Kelly Younger (kellyyounger@me.com).

SCENES FROM AN ADULTERY © 2015 by Ronan Noone. Reprinted by permission of Mark Orsini, Bret Adams Ltd. For performance rights, contact Mark Orsini (morsini@bretadamsltd.net).

SEX CELLS © 2015 by Anna Longaretti. Reprinted by permission of Anna Longaretti. Published by Samuel French, Inc. For performance rights, contact Samuel French, Inc., (212-206-8990), (www.samuelfrench.com).

SKINLESS © 2013 by Johnna Adams. Reprinted by permission of Bruce Ostler, Bret Adams Ltd. For performance rights, contact Bruce Ostler (bostler@bretadamsltd.net).

SMOKE © 2014 by Kim Davies. Reprinted by permission of Lysna Marzani, Playscripts, Inc. Published by Playscripts, Inc. For performance rights, contact Playscripts, Inc. (www.playscripts.com).

SOLDIER'S HEART © 2013 by Tammy Ryan. Reprinted by permission of Susan Gurman, Susan Gurman Agency. For performance rights, contact Susan Gurman (susan@gurmanagency.com).

SPARK © 2014 by Caridad Svich. Reprinted by permission of Elaine Devlin, Elaine Devlin Literary, Inc. For performance rights, contact Elaine Devlin (edevlinlit@aol.com).

SPRAWL © 2014 by Joshua Conkel. Reprinted by permission of Jared Weber, ICM Partners. For performance rights, contact Di Glazer, ICM Partners (dglazer@icmpartners.com).

STALKING THE BOGEYMAN © 2014 by Markus Potter. Reprinted by permission of Joseph Rosswog, Daryl Roth Theatrical Licensing. For performance rights, contact Joseph Rosswog (inquiry@darylrothlicensing.com).

TALES FROM RED VIENNA © 2013 by David Grimm. Reprinted by permission of Jared Weber, ICM Partners. Published by Dramatists Play Service. For performance rights, contact Dramatists Play Service, 440 Park Ave. S., New York, NY 10016 (www.dramatists.com) (212-683-8960).

TAR BEACH © 2014 by Tammy Ryan. Reprinted by permission of Susan Gurman, Susan Gurman Agency. For performance rights, contact Susan Gurman (susan@gurmanagency.com).

TOO MUCH SUN © 2014 by Nicky Silver. Reprinted by permission of Amy Hasselbeck, William Morris Endeavor. Published by Dramatists Play Service. For performance rights, contact Dramatists Play Service, 440 Park Ave. S., New York, NY 10016 (www.dramatists.com) (212-683-8960).

TOO TOO SOLID FLESH © 2014 by Peter M. Floyd. Reprinted by permission of Peter M. Floyd, Published by Smith and Kraus, Inc. in *2015 The Best 10-Minute Plays*. For performance rights, contact Peter M. Floyd (pmfloyd01@gmail.com).

VEILS © 2014 by Tom Coash. Reprinted by permission of Tom Coash. For performance rights, contact Tom Coash (thomascoash@sbcglobal.net).

VERONA © 2014 by Don Nigro. Reprinted by permission of Don Nigro. The entire text has been published by Applause Theatre & Cinema Books in *25 10-Minute Plays for Kids*. For performance rights, contact Samuel French, Inc., (212-206-8990), (www.samuelfrench.com).

WARM ENOUGH FOR SWIMMING © 2014 by Maggie Cino. Reprinted by permission of Maggie Cino. For performance rights, contact Maggie Cino (maggiecino@yahoo.com).

WEEK © 2014 by Barry Eitel. Reprinted by permission of Barry Eitel. For performance rights, contact Barry Eitel (barry.eitel@gmail.com).

WHITE GUY ON THE BUS © 2014 by Bruce Graham. Reprinted by permission of Alexis Williams, Bret Adams Ltd. For performance rights, contact Alexis Williams (awilliams@bretadamsltd.net).